Advent Poetry

A Journey Through Hope, Peace, Joy, and Love

Rev. Dr. Scott Tilley

Advent Poetry

Cover design © Scott Tilley

Dividers designed by Freepik

Published by Precious Poetry

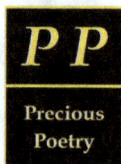

P P

Precious
Poetry

An imprint of Precious Publishing, LLC

Precious Publishing
www.PreciousPublishing.biz

ISBN-13: 978-1-951750-15-2
ISBN-13: 978-1-951750-16-9 (ebook)

TABLE OF CONTENTS

Dedication v

Preface vii

A Guide to Your Advent Journey ix

Acknowledgments xi

Week 1: Hope 1

Day 1: Dawn 3

Day 2: Candle 9

Day 3: First Snow 15

Day 4: Winter Fire 21

Day 5: Star 27

Day 6: Journey... 33

Day 7: Seedling.. 39

Week 2: Peace 45

Day 8: Stillness 47

Day 9: Quiet Waters..................................... 53

Day 10: Gentle Breeze.................................. 59

Day 11: Harmony 65

Day 12: Comfort... 71

Day 13: Refuge 77

Day 14: Moonlit Night.................................. 83

Week 3: Joy 89

Day 15: Laughter 91

Day 16: Music.. 97

Day 17: Dance 103

Day 18: Golden Light................................ 109

Day 19: Shared Feast............................... 115

Day 20: Festive Spirit............................... 121

Day 21: Starry Skies.................................. 127

Week 4: Love 133

Day 22: Family.. 135

Day 23: Warm Embrace 141

Day 24: Selfless Gift................................. 147

Christmas 153

Birth of Light.. 155

Final Light 161

Scott Tilley.. 163

Precious Poetry 165

DEDICATION

For those who long for hope, peace, joy, and love—this book is for you. May it remind you of the light we all carry within, waiting to shine brightly.

A Prayer for Advent

To the light that shines through every night,
To the hope that dawns with morning's sight.
To peace, joy, and love that ever endure,
This journey is yours — steadfast and pure.

Carrying Light Forward

Who has been a light in your life?
How can you carry that light forward?

* * *

PREFACE

Advent is a season of anticipation, reflection, and quiet hope. As the days grow shorter and the year draws to a close, this sacred time invites us to pause and prepare for Christmas and the renewal of light and love within ourselves. It is a journey that encourages us to find stillness amid the rush, to kindle light in the darkness, and to carry its warmth into the world.

This collection revolves around the themes of Advent—Hope, Peace, Joy, and Love—woven together through poetry. Poetry speaks to the soul in ways that prose cannot, offering vivid imagery, emotional depth, and moments of reflection. Each poem in this book invites you to experience Advent as both a personal and communal journey, connecting heart and spirit through the power of language and imagination.

Advent Poetry celebrates the season's essence and invites us to embrace its gifts. Whether read in solitude or shared with loved ones, these pages reflect the light we all carry within. May they inspire you to nurture that light, let it grow, and share its brilliance well beyond the days ahead

Scott Tilley
Melbourne, FL
November 28, 2024

Preparing the Heart

What does Advent mean to you?

How do you prepare your heart during this season?

* * *

A GUIDE TO YOUR ADVENT JOURNEY

This Advent book is thoughtfully organized to guide you through a meaningful journey of hope, peace, joy, and love, culminating in the celebration of Christmas. Each day presents carefully curated elements designed to inspire reflection, encourage stillness, and deepen spiritual connection.

Weekly Structure: The book is divided into four weeks, each centered on one of Advent's traditional themes: **Hope**, **Peace**, **Joy**, and **Love**. At the start of each week, you will find:

- An **evocative image** and a **complimentary poem** to introduce the theme.

- A **thematic phrase** (e.g., "Anticipation" for *Week 1: Hope*) that captures the essence of the week.

- A **brief explanation** of the week's focus and an invitation to engage with its message.

These elements set the tone for the following days, offering inspiration and context for the week's reflections.

Daily Structure: Each day in this collection unfolds around a specific theme (e.g., *Day 1: Dawn*), offering carefully chosen elements to deepen your Advent experience. From meaningful quotes to reflective poems, each component invites you into the day's meditation. Personal reflection space encourages you to make the journey your own, while a special "Bridge to Tomorrow" section connects each day's insights to the next dawn. The daily elements include:

- **Quote**: Words of wisdom chosen to frame your day.

- **Image**: Visual art that illuminates the day's theme.

- **Opening Verse**: A single stanza that sets the contemplative tone.

- **Daily Poems**: Three poems (Morning, Afternoon, Evening) invite you to pause and connect with the theme throughout the day.

- **Scripture**: A Bible verse that anchors the day's theme in sacred text.

- **Your Reflections**: Space to write down your personal thoughts, prayers, and insights.

- **Bridge to Tomorrow**: A closing meditation that includes a haiku, historical insight, and invitation, helping you carry the day's theme into tomorrow's dawn.

Final Light: The book concludes with a section titled "Final Light." This coda ties together the themes of Advent and inspires and encourages readers, reminding them to carry the light of this season into the days ahead.

* * *

Whether you use this book as a personal devotional, a guide for family reflections, or a companion during Advent, it is designed to bring light, hope, and peace into your season.

ACKNOWLEDGMENTS

Creating *Advent Poetry* has been a journey of reflection, creativity, and gratitude. This book would not exist without the inspiration drawn from the timeless themes of Advent—Hope, Peace, Joy, and Love—and the enduring light they bring to our lives.

This collection was especially inspired by the loss of my mother on October 11, 2024. Her unwavering love, guidance, and faith have been a source of light in my life, and this book is a testament to her memory and the hope she instilled in me. In her passing, I learned to embrace the quiet grace of letting go and allowing life to unfold as it must.

I sincerely thank those who have supported and encouraged me throughout this process. Your love and kindness have been my steady light, and I thank my family, friends, and spiritual community. To all who have walked this Advent journey in their own lives, thank you for showing that even the smallest light can brighten the darkest night.

Finally, to you, the reader: thank you for opening your heart to this collection. May it bring you moments of peace, joy, and inspiration as you prepare for the light of Christmas.

With Gratitude

Pause to honor those who shaped your journey.
Write their names here in gratitude.

* * *

Hope

The sky awakens, soft and wide,
Light whispers where shadows hide.
A promise blooms, the dark undone,
Hope begins with the rising sun.

Anticipation

Hope

Hope is the foundation of Advent, the quiet light that stirs within us and guides us through the longest nights. It is the anticipation of what is to come, the belief in new beginnings and brighter days, even when the present feels dark. Like a single candle piercing the gloom, hope reassures us that we are never alone.

As we reflect on hope, we remember its transformative power. Hope does not ignore life's struggles; it gives us the courage to face them with faith and perseverance. It whispers promises of renewal and reminds us that every ending carries the seeds of something new within it.

This week's readings invite you to lean into hope. Whether through the beauty of a dawn breaking, the warmth of a glowing flame, or the tender resilience of a seedling, may you find encouragement to trust in what is unseen. Let the light of hope shine brightly within your heart.

Begin this week's journey of hope…

DAY 1: DAWN

This is a wonderful day. I've never seen this one before.

—Maya Angelou

The light returns, a gentle flame,
Its quiet glow, both sure and tame.
Dawn's soft embrace bids night farewell,
A whisper of hope, its story to tell.

DAY 1: DAWN

Morning

First light breaks through the winter horizon's edge,
Like an unspoken promise carried on dawn air,
Frost-touched dewdrops hold universes waiting,
While moments swell with bright possibility,
Hope stirring beneath December's sleeping ground.

The world unfolds, one breath following another,
As lingering stars fade to brightening depths,
Their light echoing creation's earliest dawn,
When radiance first spoke through formless void,
Setting time flowing toward this awakening.

Light streams across the transforming landscape,
As night's shadows yield to approaching day,
Every sunbeam heralding what's yet to come,
Making the veiled world gradually known,
Earth's testimony written in dawn's script.

Sunrise clothes the horizon in amber fire,
Touching the waiting earth with new warmth,
Showing how darkness always gives way,
How hope renews with each winter dawn,
Writing fresh chapters in light's long story.

* * *

DAY 1: DAWN

Afternoon

Sunlight bathes the landscape in liquid gold,
Filtering through ice-glazed branches to earth,
Time flowing sweet and slow as warmed honey,
Shadows painting themselves in purple depths
Beneath December's patient, bare-limbed trees.

The day unfolds its quiet, thoughtful story,
Each passing hour a chapter in the telling
Of light's long journey toward evening's peace,
Sun-warmed stones holding memories of morning,
While afternoon wind carries whispers of what's to come.

Nature's cathedral stands open to December sky,
Its walls crafted of light and leaf-filtered air,
Every breath becoming a prayer of gratitude
For this moment, this grace, this gathered light
That fills our waiting world with golden promise.

Hope dances through dust motes in slanting rays,
Teaching us again the art of patient waiting,
Knowing each moment carries precious seeds
Of tomorrow's joy scattered on gentle breezes,
Taking root in winter's fertile, frozen soil.

* * *

DAY 1: DAWN

Evening

Twilight spreads its encompassing darkness,
The December sky awash in lavender and rose,
Day exhales its final breath into deepening dusk,
While Earth drinks deeply of the fading light,
Grateful for each sparkling moment given.

The evening stars begin their slow unveiling dance,
Each one a celestial guardian of approaching night,
Standing watch over our world settling to rest,
Their silent, ancient vigil a continuing hymn of hope,
Each glimmering point a promise of dawn's return.

The lengthening shadows grow bold in their dance,
Filling spaces where the sun's warmth lingered,
Yet they bring no fear to December's evening,
For their depths hold echoes of remembered light,
Memories that whisper through approaching dark.

As the sky deepens to winter twilight's velvet,
Our hearts recognize the presence of perfect peace,
Hope whispers its gentle goodnight to waiting Earth,
Not as an ending but as a seed deeply planted,
Waiting for tomorrow's light to call it forth again.

* * *

DAY 1: DAWN

"The steadfast love of the LORD never ceases; his mercies never come to an end; they are new every morning."

Lamentations 3:22-23

Reflections on the Day's Theme

_____

_____

_____

_____

_____

_____

_____

_____

_____

_____

_____

_____

* * *

DAY 1: DAWN

Bridge to Tomorrow

First light breaks the dawn
Morning spreads its golden wings
Promise fills the air

Advent Insight

In ancient Christian traditions, each day began at sunset rather than sunrise, teaching that light always emerges from darkness. This practice reminded the faithful that hope often begins in darkness, just as Advent starts in winter's deepest night but leads us toward Christmas dawn.

Tomorrow's Call

Before you sleep tonight, place something meaningful—a candle, a book of prayers, or a favorite mug—where dawn's first light will touch it tomorrow. Let this intentional preparation remind you how hope often begins in darkness.

#

DAY 2: CANDLE

It is better to light a candle than to curse the darkness.

—Eleanor Roosevelt

A single flame, so small, so bright,
It pierces through the darkest night.
Its steady glow, a beacon clear,
A sign of hope that draws us near.

DAY 2: CANDLE

Morning

A single flame dances through winter's early darkness,
Its unwavering glow in hushed talk with shadows,
In these uncertain moments before dawn's awakening,
The candle's warmth reveals how hope first kindles:
A small, determined light refusing surrender.

The candle's radiance transforms morning walls,
Drawing intricate patterns like light-woven stories,
We cup careful hands around this precious flame,
Learning once again how to shelter hope's first spark,
How to nurture its delicate strength through shadows.

Outside, the winter sun begins its measured climb,
But here in this circle of flickering amber light,
We remember those who walked these paths before,
Their flames burning bright through history's depths,
Their courage marking trails we follow still.

Morning brightens beyond frost-touched windows,
Yet still the candle burns with quiet purpose,
Teaching us that even in abundance of light,
We need these small, brave flames to guide us,
To show how hope persists through changing seasons.

* * *

DAY 2: CANDLE

Afternoon

December sunlight fills each room like molten gold,
While the steadfast candle holds its measured light,
Its flame unwavering against surrounding brightness,
Showing how humble beacons shine most deeply,
Speaking wisdom through the heart of passing hours.

Time flows with the rhythm of warming winter wax,
Moving from bright moment to bright moment,
Each hour marked by the candle's faithful dance,
Each flicker becoming a lesson in persistence,
On the quiet art of burning clear and true.

The flame bows gently with each passing breath,
But keeps unbroken its covenant with light,
Teaching through its incandescent endurance
How hope maintains its watch through brightest days,
Even when the world burns fierce and bright.

The contemplative hours draw us ever deeper,
As we witness the mingling of different lights:
Sunlight streaming through frost-touched windows,
While candle flame rises like wordless prayer,
Both illuminating paths toward approaching dusk.

* * *

DAY 2: CANDLE

Evening

As daylight softens into approaching winter dusk,
The candle's flame grows gradually more commanding,
Its light becoming a bridge between different worlds,
Between the fading day and the gathering darkness,
Between all that has been and what still might become.

Each separate flame becomes a treasured companion now,
Gathering at frost-touched windows and waiting tables,
Creating islands of gentle, inviting illumination
Where evening shadows pool around protected edges,
Like rising tide-waters of approaching winter night.

The deepening evening air holds countless stories of light:
Sunset colors folding themselves into precious memory,
While stars emerge overhead like distant points of hope,
And here, close at hand, candles flicker with presence,
Each one a tangible promise we can reach out and touch.

In this gathering darkness we remember ancient wisdom:
How many small flames it takes to hold back the night,
How hope spreads from one bright wick to another,
From heart to waiting heart, until winter's darkness
Becomes a field of living light, boundless and bright.

* * *

DAY 2: CANDLE

"You are the light of the world. A city set on a hill cannot be hidden."

Matthew 5:14

Reflections on the Day's Theme

* * *

13

DAY 2: CANDLE

Bridge to Tomorrow

Small flame stands guard now
Through deepening evening shade
Tomorrow's light waits

Advent Insight

The ancient tradition of vigil candles has its roots in monasteries, where a single flame would burn through the night—a quiet beacon of prayer and welcome. This "watching light" carries deep meaning. It symbolizes a steadfast hope transcending sight, reminding us that our waiting is never in vain, even in the shadows. As the candle burns, it speaks of readiness, hospitality, and the quiet faith that light can guide the weary and lost.

Tomorrow's Call

Before lighting any candle tomorrow, hold it for a moment and consider its potential—not yet aflame, but ready to bring light. Choose a specific person or situation to keep in your thoughts as you light the flame, allowing your intention to bridge the gap between hope and action.

# # #

DAY 3: FIRST SNOW

Kindness is like snow—it beautifies everything it covers.

—Kahlil Gibran

Each flake descends, a whispered song,
A quiet grace that won't stay long.
The earth is hushed, its breath held tight,
Hope awakens in winter's white.

DAY 3: FIRST SNOW

Morning

Dawn unfolds across a world completely transformed,
Each familiar shape made wondrously new again
By the first snow's silent, unexpected blessing,
Pristine whiteness stretching toward far horizons
Like pages of possibility waiting for their story.

Winter light sparkles across untouched morning drifts,
Each crystal becoming a prism of endless possibility,
While the December air holds its breath in wonder
At this baptism of whiteness blessing the world,
This cleansing transformation of ordinary space.

Morning shadows paint themselves in deepest blue
Against the canvas of freshly fallen winter snow,
While early birds leave their delicate signatures,
Their tracks becoming careful morning calligraphy
Written across nature's newly offered blank page.

In this hushed and sacred morning meditation,
We witness earth's unexpected transformation,
How grace can fall so softly through darkness
Yet completely transform everything it touches,
Teaching us again hope's endless possibilities.

* * *

DAY 3: FIRST SNOW

Afternoon

Sunlight dances across snow-laden winter branches,
Creating constellations of unexpected brilliance,
The afternoon air shimmering with diamond light,
As if joy itself had become suddenly visible,
Scattered across our waiting, transformed world.

Children's bright laughter rings through crystal air
As they discover winter's unexpected treasures:
The perfect snowball waiting to be formed,
Each fresh track marking new exploration,
Their breath making clouds that float toward heaven.

Snow continues its quiet work of transformation,
Smoothing every edge, softening familiar sounds,
Until the afternoon world becomes completely new,
Wrapped in layers of wonder and possibility,
Each moment precious in its perfect stillness.

Even as lengthening shadows stretch blue fingers,
The snow holds captured light within its depths,
Glowing with remembered morning sunshine,
Showing us how hope persists through darkness,
Even as the shortened day begins its fading.

* * *

DAY 3: FIRST SNOW

Evening

Twilight transforms the snow to iridescent pearl,
Each drift becoming a gentle wave of captured light
In the deepening tide of approaching evening,
Stars emerging to find their perfect reflections
Scattered across the hushed and waiting earth.

The snow-blessed world feels smaller somehow,
Wrapped securely in its blanket of white silence,
Yet paradoxically larger in its transformation,
As if the snow has erased all mortal boundaries
Between our earth and the star-scattered sky.

Porch lights cast their golden welcoming pools
Across evening snow still pristine and untouched,
While windows glow like warm ember beacons,
Each one offering sanctuary and belonging
Against the gathering winter darkness beyond.

In this completely transformed evening landscape,
We learn again the deepest lessons about hope:
How it falls as softly as snow through darkness,
Until the world we thought we fully understood
Becomes a place of wonder and new beginning.

* * *

DAY 3: FIRST SNOW

"Though your sins are like scarlet, they shall be as white as snow."

Isaiah 1:18

Reflections on the Day's Theme

_____

_____

_____

_____

_____

_____

_____

_____

_____

_____

_____

_____

* * *

DAY 3: FIRST SNOW

Bridge to Tomorrow

White blankets settle
Earth holds breath in wonder now
Dawn will paint it gold

<u>Advent Insight</u>

In Nordic Christian culture, the first snow of winter is often seen as a gentle reminder of the season's sacredness, its pure white blanket echoing themes of purification and grace before Christmas. It's easy to imagine communities gathering for "snow vigils," marveling at the quiet beauty of falling snow and sharing stories of hope and renewal around the hearth. Each snowflake, unique and fleeting, seems to carry whispers of divine wonder, reminding everyone of the grace woven into the fabric of creation.

<u>Tomorrow's Call</u>

Find something familiar transformed by time or circumstance—perhaps a leaf pressed in a book or a photograph from years past. Place it where you'll see it tomorrow, letting it remind you how beauty often comes through transformation.

# # #

DAY 4: WINTER FIRE

Keep a little fire burning; however small, however hidden.

—Cormac McCarthy

A fire burns, its embers glow,
A warmth within, while cold winds blow.
Its gentle heat, a gift of grace,
A light that shines in every space.

DAY 4: WINTER FIRE

Morning

The hearth awakens slowly from night's slumber,
Embers stirring beneath their blanket of gray ash
Like ancient memories of yesterday's warmth waiting,
Fresh kindling catches the first promising spark,
And morning's flames begin their sacred dance anew.

The fire speaks to us in its primordial language,
Crackling stories of light and heat through ages,
Of deep caverns where our ancestors first gathered,
First learned to cherish flame's transforming power,
First kindled hope against overwhelming darkness.

Morning shadows retreat before the growing warmth,
While early sunlight streams through frosted glass
To join the firelight in blessing this sacred space,
Two kinds of radiance merging in quiet triumph,
Teaching us again how darkness yields to light.

We gather close within this circle of promised warmth,
Adding fuel carefully to feed the strengthening flame,
Learning once more how hope grows from small sparks:
One ember, tenderly nurtured against the cold,
Until its warmth fills every corner of our waiting world.

* * *

DAY 4: WINTER FIRE

Afternoon

The fire settles into its steady winter burning,
Each log surrendering slowly to transformation
While afternoon light spills through tall windows,
Painting paths of gold across the quieting room,
Two different warmths embracing winter's chill.

Shadows perform their ancient dance on watching walls,
Their patterns telling stories of light's endless journey,
Of its perpetual conversation with approaching darkness,
Teaching us through flame how hope flickers bright
But never fully fades from memory or promise.

The deepening afternoon grows warmer still,
As flames speak their gentle winter wisdom
About patience, about faithful endurance,
About how light prevails through longest nights
By burning steady and true through darkness.

Time drifts like woodsmoke through sunbeams,
Each moment caught in that gentle ascension
Between earth's flame and heaven's light,
While the fire reminds us how grace arrives
To warm even the coldest winter afternoon.

* * *

DAY 4: WINTER FIRE

Evening

Night presses thick against frost-touched windows
While the fire burns ever more bright and welcoming,
Drawing us closer to its pulsing, faithful heart
Where orange flames leap in joyful celebration,
Like prayers made visible in winter's darkness.

Each different wood adds its particular music:
Pine sings high and sweet through winter air,
Oak maintains the steady rhythm of burning,
While cedar releases its ancient fragrant incense
Into the gathering darkness of December night.

The fire creates its own complete universe,
A sphere of light and transforming warmth
Where stories find their perfect expression,
Where hearts draw close in understanding,
Where hope burns steady through longest night.

In this sacred circle of firelight's blessing,
We remember again our deepest identity:
Keepers of the flame through winter darkness,
Guardians of hope's eternal bright promise,
Bearers of light that warms the waiting world.

* * *

DAY 4: WINTER FIRE

"For our God is a consuming fire."

Hebrews 12:29

Reflections on the Day's Theme

* * *

DAY 4: WINTER FIRE

Bridge to Tomorrow

Hearth flames dance and leap
Stories told in warmth and light
Morning waits its turn

Advent Insight

The Yule log tradition in medieval Europe intertwined ancient folk customs with Christian themes. During the longest nights of winter, a carefully selected log, often blessed and ceremonially lit, was burned, its glowing embers symbolizing light and hope amid darkness. Some communities kept the ashes or embers to start the following year's fire, creating an unbroken chain of warmth and promise—a reminder of enduring grace through winters past and future.

Tomorrow's Call

Set aside kindling for tomorrow's light—a literal candle, a beloved psalm, or a treasured memory. Just as building a fire requires preparation, allow this intentional gathering to become part of your chain of hope stretching forward.

#

DAY 5: STAR

For my part I know nothing with any certainty, but the sight of the stars makes me dream.

—Vincent van Gogh

Above the night, a star takes flight,
A steady guide, its glow so bright.
It calls the lost with gentle grace,
To seek the light, to find their place.

DAY 5: STAR

Morning

The morning star stands eternal sentinel overhead,
Last brilliant guardian in the brightening winter sky,
Holding its sacred place as dawn approaches gently,
Like hope maintaining its vigil through darkest hours,
Even as night's shadows yield to approaching day.

Ancient starlight continues its patient journey still,
Crossing unimaginable distances through deep time
To touch our waiting world with celestial blessing,
Teaching us how promises made in ages past
Continue to light our paths through winter darkness.

The star's pure radiance mingles with breaking dawn,
A gentle reminder that guidance comes in many forms,
That hope sometimes shines most bright and clear
Just before day breaks through winter's darkness,
When we think our waiting has lasted forever.

As morning gradually claims the transforming sky,
We carry the star's bright message in our hearts:
How it pierced through depths of endless darkness,
How it marked the path toward promised morning,
How it leads us still toward hope's perfect light.

* * *

DAY 5: STAR

Afternoon

Though stars hide themselves in December daylight,
Their presence guides us still through winter hours,
Like hope working unseen beneath life's surface,
Through all our days of doubting and certainty,
Constant despite temporary earthly obscurity.

The sun's path traces ancient astral stories still,
Written in starlight older than human memory,
Reminding us how seekers have always found ways
Through darkness toward light, through doubt to faith,
By lifting their eyes toward heaven's guidance.

Each bright afternoon holds evening's promise,
When stars will return to their appointed places,
Teaching us how patient waiting creates its own light,
Its own form of guidance through winter darkness,
Its own testament to hope's eternal return.

Even in these brightest moments of winter day,
Stars continue their stately, measureless journey,
Moving in cosmic dance beyond our seeing,
Weaving patterns of promise across infinite space,
Above our small world wrapped in December light.

* * *

Day 5: Star

Evening

First evening stars emerge like whispered promises,
Piercing through twilight's deepening purple veil
With points of ancient, ever-burning radiance,
Each one opening a window into infinite space
Where hope shines eternal through darkness.

The winter evening sky deepens to perfect black,
Becoming fields of innumerable scattered lights,
While constellations tell their ageless stories
Of guidance through wilderness and stormy seas,
Of journeys beginning and blessed returns home.

Each star burns with its own determined purpose,
A steadfast beacon piercing cosmic darkness,
Teaching us through its ancient, faithful presence
How distance cannot diminish light's true power
When hope remains constant through longest night.

Night spreads its velvet darkness across heaven
Beneath these countless celestial diamonds,
While we stand in wonder beneath winter stars,
Learning again how light always finds its way
Through seemingly endless fields of darkness.

* * *

DAY 5: STAR

"When they saw the star, they rejoiced … with great joy."

Matthew 2:10

Reflections on the Day's Theme

_____

_____

_____

_____

_____

_____

_____

_____

_____

_____

_____

_____

_____

_____

_____

_____

_____

* * *

DAY 5: STAR

Bridge to Tomorrow

Night stars guide our way
Ancient light speaks through darkness
Dawn waits patiently

Advent Insight

The Star of Bethlehem has long symbolized more than guidance—it represents hope's enduring brilliance amid darkness. For early Christians, every star in the heavens echoed the memory of that first celestial herald, a reminder that divine light reaches us across great distances and time, arriving precisely when we need it most. In its glow, they saw the promise of God's presence breaking through the night.

Tomorrow's Call

Select a direction that holds special significance—maybe east towards the dawn or north towards the steadfast star. Before you sleep tonight, turn toward this direction and set an intention for tomorrow, allowing the starlight to connect the time between evening and morning hope.

# # #

DAY 6: JOURNEY

The journey of a thousand miles begins with a single step.

—Lao Tzu

Each step ahead, a path unknown,
Through winding ways, we're never alone.
The journey calls, and faith inspires,
A heart alight with sacred fires.

DAY 6: JOURNEY

Morning

Morning mist parts like ancient temple veils,
Revealing the untrodden path stretching before us,
Each frost-touched step promising new beginnings
On this timeless pilgrimage through December days,
This sacred journey of seeking and becoming whole.

Winter frost edges our waiting trail with brilliance,
Each crystal catching early light's pure blessing,
While morning birds trace their graceful paths
Across the gradually brightening winter sky,
Showing countless ways toward approaching light.

The winter sun rises steadily behind our shoulders,
Casting long shadows that point forever forward
Like nature's compass showing unknown paths,
Teaching us how hope moves through darkness
Always toward the beckoning horizon's call.

We shoulder our questions like precious bundles,
Pack our dreams like provisions for the journey,
And step into morning's transforming light,
Knowing every pilgrimage through darkness
Begins with this one sacred, courageous step.

* * *

Day 6: Journey

Afternoon

The winter path unfolds beneath searching feet
Like an ancient story gradually being written,
Each measured mile becoming a meditation
On distance and desire through passing time,
On how far hope can carry weary travelers.

December shadows walk beside us now as friends,
Companions on this unexpected journey forward,
While overhead, clouds drift through endless blue
Like fellow pilgrims showing by their passage
How light moves constantly through time and space.

The afternoon sun warms our bent shoulders,
Blessing each determined step toward horizon
With golden encouragement through winter air,
While distant hills beckon with strange promise
Of discoveries and wonders yet unknown.

We pause to mark our progress through the day,
Not by counted miles but by precious moments:
Each breath becoming a small arrival home,
Each heartbeat moving us ever closer still
Toward whatever light calls us forward now.

* * *

DAY 6: JOURNEY

Evening

As daylight fades to winter twilight shadows,
Our journey's pace grows quiet and reflective,
Like a snow-fed river finding eventual stillness
After rapids, teaching tired travelers wisdom
About when to rest and when to press forward.

Stars emerge like ancient waymarks overhead,
Timeless guides appearing at their appointed time
To chart our evening course through darkness,
The same eternal lights that led countless others
Through sacred nights of seeking and finding.

We make camp in this space between moments,
Between all that was and what still might be,
Finding in our bone-deep weariness tonight
A deeper kind of strength we never expected,
A more enduring hope than morning promised.

Night wraps around our shoulders like blessing,
Like a pilgrim's well-worn cloak of comfort,
While dreams trace tomorrow's waiting path,
Reminding us that the journey itself becomes
Our deepest blessing through winter darkness.

* * *

DAY 6: JOURNEY

"The LORD will keep your going out and your coming in from this time forth and forevermore."

Psalm 121:8

Reflections on the Day's Theme

_____

_____

_____

_____

_____

_____

_____

_____

_____

_____

_____

_____

_____

_____

* * *

DAY 6: JOURNEY

Bridge to Tomorrow

Footsteps mark the snow
Each print tells where we have been
Path leads ever on

Advent Insight

While medieval pilgrims undertook their journeys throughout the year, Advent often deepened their sense of purpose, echoing the sacred journey of Mary and Joseph to Bethlehem. Each step embodied faith and anticipation for these travelers, aligning with the season's themes of waiting and hope. They measured their progress not in miles but through the quiet discoveries of the heart—moments of grace that guided them as reliably as any star.

Tomorrow's Call

Place a small stone or token in a spot where you'll find it in the morning. Let it symbolize a step in your journey—not just physical movement, but spiritual growth. Tomorrow, carry it with you as a reminder that every journey begins with the renewal of hope.

# # #

DAY 7: SEEDLING

The creation of a thousand forests is in one acorn.

—Ralph Waldo Emerson

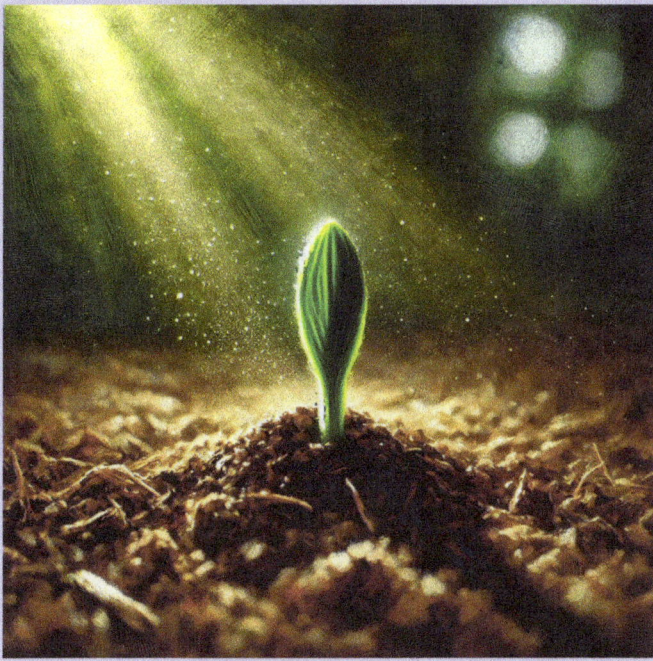

A seedling grows, so small, so new,
With roots unseen, yet strong and true.
Its fragile form holds boundless might,
A living hope, a source of light.

DAY 7: SEEDLING

Morning

Deep beneath winter's frost-touched morning earth,
A seedling stirs with unexpected determination,
Breaking resolutely through its protective shell
In complete darkness, reaching ever upward
Through layers of frozen soil toward distant light.

No mortal eye witnesses this courageous work,
This first brave push toward promised spring,
While sacred ground holds its precious secrets,
And underground networks of ancient roots
Share whispered messages of becoming more.

Morning frost traces temporary patterns above
Where this hidden miracle unfolds in darkness,
Where tender roots begin their patient journey
Through fertile depths of winter-waiting soil
Toward spring's distant but certain promise.

The strengthening sun touches frozen ground,
Gradually warming earth's dreaming places
Where countless seeds cradle future gardens,
Each one knowing perfectly its appointed season,
Patient with infinite green possibilities.

* * *

DAY 7: SEEDLING

Afternoon

Winter sunlight warms the deep-waiting soil
Where tomorrow's gardens grow unseen still,
Each small seed holding spring's complete promise
Within its tender, perfectly crafted heart,
While December winds sweep frozen fields.

Time moves in spirals through winter gardens
Where summer's flowers sleep beneath snow,
Their next blooming already written clearly
In scattered seeds beneath barren ground,
Each one knowing its perfect moment comes.

The lengthening afternoon shelters dreams
Of green abundance in frozen winter soil,
While underground, countless miracles unfold
In darkness perfect for tender beginning,
Hope taking root in December's quiet heart.

Patient earth cradles these small prophecies
Of leaf and flower through winter afternoons,
While beneath the surface, life continues
Its ancient cycle of death and rebirth,
Each seed a promise of spring's return.

* * *

DAY 7: SEEDLING

Evening

Evening settles gently on winter's fallow ground
Where tomorrow's gardens sleep in sacred darkness,
While stars wheel overhead in stately procession,
Marking time's slow turning toward distant spring
Until earth awakens to seasonal resurrection.

Night air carries unexpected promises still
In scattered seeds drifting through twilight,
Each one bearing within its humble shell
A complete story of renewal and return,
Of hope sleeping through winter darkness.

The winter-wrapped earth never truly sleeps,
Even in the deepest heart of December night,
As seeds dream their green becoming still,
Drawing mysterious strength from frozen soil
And infinite stars wheeling bright above.

Darkness wraps the sleeping garden close,
In necessary stillness and perfect silence,
While beneath December's frozen surface,
Hope continues its quiet, patient working
Toward spring's inevitable transformation.

* * *

DAY 7: SEEDLING

"The kingdom of God is as if a man should scatter seed on the ground. He sleeps and rises night and day, and the seed sprouts and grows; he knows not how."

Mark 4:26-27

Reflections on the Day's Theme

* * *

DAY 7: SEEDLING

Bridge to Tomorrow

Deep in winter earth
Tomorrow's garden slumbers
Hope grows in the dark

Advent Insight

Throughout the Advent season, planting bulbs—such as paperwhite narcissus or amaryllis—symbolizes the quiet power of hope. Timed to bloom near Christmas, these flowers remind us that every seedling begins its journey hidden, requiring patience and trust in what cannot yet be seen. In the same way, Advent invites us to nurture faith, even when the harvest feels far away.

Tomorrow's Call

Before dawn tomorrow, choose something small that holds potential—a seed, a word, or an idea—and grant it the space to grow. Place it where it marks the boundary between what is and what might be, allowing it to serve as a reminder that hope often begins in the hidden places.

# # #

Peace

A gentle stream flows soft and still,
Its song a balm, a quiet will.
Peace settles deep, a silent grace,
Within the heart, a sacred space.

Serenity

Peace

Peace is not the absence of noise but the presence of calm amidst life's storms. It flows like quiet waters, soothing our hearts and minds when we are overwhelmed. During Advent, peace invites us to slow down, breathe deeply, and reconnect with what truly matters.

This week, we reflect on the serenity of surrendering our worries to God. Peace does not demand perfection but meets us as we are, offering solace and renewal. It is the gentle breeze that calms our spirit, the stillness that restores our strength.

This week, may you discover the beauty of peace through poems and reflections. Let it wash over you, quieting the noise of life and drawing you into the sacred space where love and understanding flourish.

Begin this week's journey of peace...

DAY 8: STILLNESS

Silence is sometimes the best answer.

—Dalai Lama

The world slows down, its chaos still,
A quiet calm, a soothing will.
In stillness deep, the heart can see,
A sacred space where peace will be.

DAY 8: STILLNESS

Morning

In the sacred space between winter heartbeats,
Before our world fully wakes to morning light,
Stillness opens its encompassing, gentle hands
Offering moments of perfect, complete peace
Into the crystalline silence of breaking dawn.

No winter wind disturbs the waiting branches,
No birds break the expectant morning quiet,
The frost-touched air holds its precious secrets
In crystalline stillness perfect and complete,
Like a pause between cosmic heartbeats.

The December sun rises without sound or hurry,
Threading golden needles through frozen branches,
While nothing moves and nothing breaks silence,
The world simply becoming what it must be
In the perfect stillness of winter morning.

These hushed moments teach their ancient wisdom:
How peace dwells most deep in perfect stillness,
How silence nourishes our winter-hungry souls,
How morning's quietude feeds our deepest needs,
Standing still in time's endless flowing river.

* * *

DAY 8: STILLNESS

Afternoon

Winter clouds hang motionless in endless blue,
Fixed like monuments in December's quiet sky,
While time slows to a frozen stream's stillness,
Each moment suspended in perfect balance
Between what was and what still might be.

Fresh snow settles on bare branches without sound,
Each flake finding its appointed resting place,
While the world holds its breath in wonder,
Afternoon stillness becoming meditation,
Teaching peace through perfect quietude.

Shadows rest unmoving on untouched snow,
Even the restless wind grows contemplative,
Learning stillness from the winter-quiet earth,
Finding peace in afternoon's perfect pause,
Where nothing needs doing or becoming.

In this carved-out space of winter afternoon,
Between one breath and another's gentle taking,
Peace writes its story in perfect stillness,
Teaching us again the art of being present,
Finding rest in the heart of sacred silence.

* * *

DAY 8: STILLNESS

Evening

Evening stars emerge in profound silence now,
Each one claiming its space in infinite dark
Without fanfare or unnecessary movement,
Each point of light finding perfect placement
In winter evening's deepening quietude.

Night settles over the landscape without hurry,
Draping its star-scattered shadows so gently
Over the sleeping, snow-covered earth below,
Where no leaf stirs and no branch dares bend
In this moment of complete, perfect calm.

Peace flows like still water through darkness,
Finding its way into every shadowed space,
Filling empty corners with blessed silence,
Touching each hollow with quiet blessing,
Teaching us again about tranquil trust.

In this most sacred stillness of winter night,
We finally find our center, our true north,
Where peace dwells eternal and unchanging
In the quiet heart of deepening darkness,
Perfect silence blessing all it touches.

* * *

DAY 8: STILLNESS

"Be still, and know that I am God. I will be exalted among the nations, I will be exalted in the earth!"

Psalm 46:10

Reflections on the Day's Theme

* * *

Day 8: Stillness

Bridge to Tomorrow

Silence holds its breath
Winter mist cradles mountain
Peace speaks without words

Advent Insight

The Desert Fathers of the early church embraced "sacred silence" to encounter peace in the space between words. For them, the stillness was not an emptiness but a presence—a living, active state of receptivity that prepared the heart for divine encounters. In the quiet of Advent, we, too, are invited to dwell in this sacred stillness, attuned to the whispers of grace while preparing the heart for divine encounters.

Tomorrow's Call

Create a small sanctuary of stillness for tomorrow—a corner, a moment, a pause in your day. Mark it with something simple: a smooth stone, an empty bowl, or a single leaf. Let this space remind you that peace often begins in stillness.

# # #

DAY 9: QUIET WATERS

Water is the soul of the Earth.

—W.H. Auden

Beside the stream, where waters flow,
A gentle song begins to grow.
Its ripples speak of calm and grace,
A mirror bright, a resting place.

DAY 9: QUIET WATERS

Morning

Winter sunrise touches still waters with reverence,
Transforming mirror-smooth surfaces to burnished gold,
While no ripple breaks the profound morning calm,
Peace reflecting perfect light in nature's glass,
Heaven and earth meeting in quiet celebration.

Sacred mist rises slowly from waiting waters,
Like ancient prayers ascending through morning frost,
While the lake holds heaven's light in its depths,
Cradling dawn's fire in its winter dreaming,
Each moment a meditation on stillness.

Delicate ice edges the lake's quietest coves
Where still water meets frost-touched shore,
Creating boundaries between motion and stillness
Where peace finds its perfect reflection again,
Teaching us the beauty of quiet surrender.

Dawn continues painting the water's passive face
With ever-changing rose and amber hues unfolding,
Each color spreading unbroken across morning calm,
Nature offering its own pure meditation
On finding peace in perfect stillness.

* * *

DAY 9: QUIET WATERS

Afternoon

Winter sunlight warms the lake's dark waters
Where ancient depths hold centuries of quiet,
Fish gliding silent as thoughts through shadow,
Finding peace in their liquid winter world,
Far beneath the afternoon's bright surface.

The quiet lake mirrors December clouds above,
Creating two skies meeting in perfect stillness,
No wind disturbing their profound union
Where heaven and earth join in reflection,
Afternoon peace flowing deep as water.

Bare branches cast their shadowed calligraphy
Across the lake's untroubled winter face,
Drawing patterns of perfect stillness there,
Speaking peace through silent afternoon,
Each moment floating free of time.

Light plays across the water's gentle swells,
Each ripple catching sun then smoothing back
To glass-like calm in endless succession,
Teaching patience through quiet waters,
How peace returns to still the restless heart.

* * *

DAY 9: QUIET WATERS

Evening

Twilight settles softly on winter waters,
Spreading purple shadows impossibly deep
Into evening's contemplative heart, while
Stars prepare to find their perfect mirrors
In the lake's darkening, peaceful face.

Night approaches these quiet waters gently,
Where liquid darkness meets velvet sky
In depths of perfect understanding,
Peace flowing between different worlds
Through the gathering winter dark.

First evening stars touch the water's surface,
Their ancient light carried fathoms deep
Into territories of profound quiet
Where daylight's memories sleep undisturbed
Beneath winter water's perfect calm.

The lake cradles darkness with infinite care,
Each star finding its twin in still water
Until heaven above and heaven below
Become one in profound winter peace,
Night completing its quiet miracle.

* * *

DAY 9: QUIET WATERS

"He leads me beside still waters. He restores my soul."

Psalm 23:2-3

Reflections on the Day's Theme

_____

_____

_____

_____

_____

_____

_____

_____

_____

_____

_____

_____

* * *

DAY 9: QUIET WATERS

Bridge to Tomorrow

Still waters mirror
Heaven's light in liquid calm
Stars swim silently

Advent Insight

Medieval mystics often spoke of "waters of peace," discovering in still pools and frozen lakes a reflection of divine tranquility. They believed that just as undisturbed water settles into perfect stillness, the soul also finds its natural peace when gifted with quiet. In the quiet waters of Advent, we are invited to rest, reflect, and prepare for the flow of grace to come.

Tomorrow's Call

Fill a simple bowl with water and place it where morning light will find it. Let its surface become both mirror and meditation, reminding you tomorrow that peace, like water, can reflect heaven's light when we allow ourselves to be still.

#

DAY 10: GENTLE BREEZE

A breeze in the morning is nature's whisper.

—Unknown

A breath of air, so soft and light,
It whispers through the trees at night.
Its tender touch, a sweet reprieve,
A gift of peace for hearts that grieve.

DAY 10: GENTLE BREEZE

Morning

A gentle wind awakens the winter morning world,
Carrying whispered messages through frosted air,
While bare branches receive its tender touch,
Dancing slowly in the strengthening light
Like thoughts drifting through morning meditation.

Winter birds ride these currents of morning grace,
Finding paths written in invisible flowing script,
While the breeze speaks its quiet benediction
Through ice-touched branches and evergreen boughs,
Each movement a prayer of perfect peace.

Air moves across winter water's mirrored surface,
Drawing ripple-songs from quiet morning lakes,
Creating patterns of endless variation
That smooth themselves back to perfect calm,
Each breath bringing messages of dawn.

Morning wind carries frost on gentle wings,
Scattering diamond dust through golden light,
While peace flows through moving air
Like music too subtle for mortal ears,
Each moment a dance of stillness and motion.

* * *

DAY 10: GENTLE BREEZE

Afternoon

December clouds drift through endless blue space,
Sailing on gentle currents above winter fields,
Their shadows floating across untouched snow
Like thoughts crossing a peaceful mind,
Each movement part of nature's quiet ballet.

Dried grasses bend and rise in gentle waves,
Moving together in winter wind's soft touch,
Creating patterns across empty fields
Where peace flows through afternoon air,
Touching everything in passing blessing.

Snow lifts in occasional gentle spirals,
Catching afternoon sun in its brief dance
Before settling again to perfect rest,
While the breeze carries winter memories
Through this moment into the next.

Air moves between earth and endless sky,
Bridging worlds with its gentle presence,
Creating paths through winter stillness
Where peace flows free as breathing,
Each current carrying quiet blessing.

* * *

DAY 10: GENTLE BREEZE

Evening

Evening wind settles like a peaceful sigh,
Smoothing day's wrinkles from winter fields
While stars emerge in growing stillness,
Each one blessed by gentle movement
Of air growing quiet with approaching night.

Night breezes move with silent grace,
Carrying messages through dark branches
Written in the language of winter peace,
While shadows dance their slow pavane
Through spaces between land and sky.

Wind-songs grow gradually more gentle,
Evening settling deep into tranquil rest,
Like a child drifting toward peaceful sleep,
Air moving now like memory through trees,
Each breath a lullaby of coming peace.

December night cradles these final breezes,
Stirring winter shadows with tender touch
While peace descends with gathering dark,
Moving like thought through quiet spaces,
Between the stars and sleeping Earth.

* * *

DAY 10: GENTLE BREEZE

"The Spirit of God has made me, and the breath of the Almighty gives me life."

Job 33:4

Reflections on the Day's Theme

* * *

63

DAY 10: GENTLE BREEZE

Bridge to Tomorrow

Wind whispers secrets
Through bare December branches
Peace rides winter air

Advent Insight

In the early church, gentle winds were viewed as a symbol of the Holy Spirit's quiet and sustaining presence. During Advent, they noted how winter breezes moved softly through bare branches, reminding them that true peace often comes not in great gusts but in the gentle stirrings that barely disturb a candle's flame. In such moments, the heart becomes attuned to the rhythm of divine peace.

Tomorrow's Call

Hang a small ribbon or light scarf where tomorrow's breeze can find it. Let its gentle movement remind you that peace often arrives like a whisper, not a shout—in the spaces between moments, in the pause between breaths.

#

DAY 11: HARMONY

Harmony makes small things grow; lack of it makes great things decay.

—Sallust

The notes of life align as one,
A melody both soft and strong.
In harmony, the soul is free,
A perfect chord of unity.

DAY 11: HARMONY

Morning

Dawn orchestrates its winter symphony in silence,
Through frost-touched branches reaching skyward,
Their shadows writing music across untouched snow
While morning light conducts the flowing hours
In movements as gentle as whispered prayers.

Nature awakens note by deliberate perfect note,
Each sound finding its ordained place in sequence:
Bird song weaving through wind's soft whispers,
Ice crystals chiming against waiting branches,
Morning bells calling across hushed winter fields.

The world's voices blend in sacred counterpoint,
Deep bass notes of ancient pines standing guard
Find harmony with bright sparrow's morning song,
While dawn frost releases its delicate music,
Each sound part of winter's perfect score.

The music of morning builds with quiet grace,
Each element joining the whole in perfect time,
Through winter's carefully crafted composition,
Peace flowing through every measured phrase
Until nature's symphony achieves completion.

* * *

DAY 11: HARMONY

Afternoon

Sunlight orchestrates winter shadows' dance,
Across snow-covered fields where wind and branch
Create unexpected duets in afternoon light,
Their music flowing outward through quiet air
To bless all the listening winter world.

The day unfolds its rhythmic winter pulse
In steady heartbeats through passing time:
Snow settling with its crystalline music,
Trees swaying to their ancient rhythms,
Earth breathing its eternal quiet song.

Winter light plays subtle countermelodies
Against deeper tones of lengthening shadows,
While afternoon winds conduct their symphony
Through branches and across open spaces,
Each moment part of nature's endless score.

Sacred sound fills these December hours:
Ice singing on thawing afternoon puddles,
Ravens calling their deep notes across valleys,
All voices blending in perfect harmony
Through winter afternoon's peaceful chorus.

* * *

DAY 11: HARMONY

Evening

Night approaches with string-song gentleness,
Drawing its bow across the twilight horizon
Where evening stars begin their ancient aria,
Each constellation adding its particular voice
To winter's darkening composition of peace.

The evening world deepens its harmonic notes
Into bass tones of earth settling to rest,
While high above, planets dance their paths
Through celestial spheres' eternal melody,
Writing music across star-scattered skies.

Twilight releases its collection of evening songs:
Owl calls echoing through darkening woods,
Wind instruments playing through winter grass,
Day's final notes folding into gathering dark,
All joining night's growing symphony.

Peace flows through December darkness now
In measures marked by starlight and shadow,
As evening gathers all sounds unto itself,
Weaving separate voices into one song,
Night's harmony becoming complete at last.

* * *

DAY 11: HARMONY

"Live in harmony with one another."

Romans 12:16

Reflections on the Day's Theme

* * *

DAY 11: HARMONY

Bridge to Tomorrow

Notes blend and weave peace
Winter winds join bird song now
Dawn's sweet symphony

Advent Insight

In medieval monasteries, the practice of "sacred harmony" during Advent extended to daily tasks, which were performed in rhythmic unity. Bell ringers synchronized their timing so that nearby churches produced overlapping tones, creating a rich tapestry of sound. This practice reminded them—and reminds us—that peace emerges when diverse voices unite for a common purpose and resonate as one.

Tomorrow's Call

Select three distinct sounds in your surroundings—maybe a bell, a breath, and a birdsong—and observe how they intertwine. Allow this awareness to carry into tomorrow, reminding you that peace often arises from combining seemingly unrelated elements.

# # #

DAY 12: COMFORT

What can we do but keep on breathing in and out, modest and willing, and in our places?

—Mary Oliver

Beneath the weight of life's demands,
A quiet strength will take your hands.
Its tender touch, a warm embrace,
A shelter found, a holy space.

DAY 12: COMFORT

Morning

Winter morning wraps gentle warmth around us,
Like a well-loved blanket cherished through years,
While steam rises from morning cups of comfort
Into frost-touched air that fills December dawn,
Each breath bringing solace to early hours.

Sunlight spills across time-worn wooden floors,
Through windows wearing delicate lace frost,
Finding all the quiet corners where peace dwells
In familiar shapes of cherished belongings:
Old chair, hearth stones, grandmother's quilt.

Morning rituals unfold with practiced grace,
Each following treasured family rhythms:
Kettle's whistle piercing morning quiet,
Radio murmuring its familiar comfort,
Each small sound anchoring the awakening day.

Our home holds its gathered warmth within,
Like a sanctuary against winter morning,
Each room offering its particular shelter
From the world's wild and restless weather,
Peace dwelling deep in these simple spaces.

* * *

DAY 12: COMFORT

Afternoon

Outside, winter winds prowl the garden paths,
But here, wrapped in afternoon's embrace,
Old wood and warm stone shelter memories
Where generations have found their comfort,
Peace seeping gentle through every wall.

December sun pours honey-gold through glass,
Past wavering panes worked thin by time,
Touching familiar photographs with grace,
Worn books, collected treasures, loved things,
Each one holding stories of belonging.

The house cat curls in her chosen sunbeam,
While radiators hum their metal lullabies,
And somewhere in the quiet kitchen depths
Yesterday's soup simmers on slow heat,
Filling every corner with scents of home.

Time moves differently within these walls,
Measured not in minutes but peaceful moments
Between heartbeats and quiet breaths,
Where winter cannot reach with frozen hands,
Safe in afternoon's sheltering embrace.

* * *

DAY 12: COMFORT

Evening

Night draws its curtain early across the sky,
While inside, lamps bloom in familiar corners,
Spreading pools of gentle golden comfort
Through rooms where evening peace gathers
Like a blessing on the close of day.

The last light retreats beyond frosted glass,
As cherished shadows find their evening places
Among the furnishings of our quiet lives,
Each darkness welcome as an old friend,
Comfort dwelling deep in winter night.

Small lights stand guard against the dark:
Reading lamp, hearth fire, candle flame,
Stars glimpsed through window glass,
Each one a gentle reminder in darkness
That light remains to guide us home.

Evening wraps us in its quiet comfort,
In well-worn peace worked smooth by years
Of nights like this, when winter wheels
Above our shelter, and home holds close
All that we most treasure in the dark.

* * *

DAY 12: COMFORT

"Come to me, all who labor and are heavy laden, and I will give you rest."

Matthew 11:28

Reflections on the Day's Theme

_____

_____

_____

_____

_____

_____

_____

_____

_____

_____

_____

* * *

DAY 12: COMFORT

Bridge to Tomorrow

Warmth wraps us in peace
Like quilts passed down through the years
Love stitched into time

Advent Insight

The German tradition of "Adventskaffee" dates back centuries, when families would gather each Sunday of Advent to share coffee, seasonal breads, and quiet conversation. These moments of comfort and connection showed that peace often arises from simple rituals shared with those we hold dear.

Tomorrow's Call

Prepare a small comfort for tomorrow—perhaps a beloved mug, a treasured book, or a cherished photograph. Put it where the morning light can find it, reminding you that peace often comes in simple moments of connection and care.

# # #

DAY 13: REFUGE

A wise man seeks shelter before the storm.

—Proverb

A cottage waits, its doors ajar,
A refuge near, no matter how far.
Within its walls, the weary rest,
A place of peace, a soul refreshed.

DAY 13: REFUGE

Morning

Snow banks rise like ramparts against stone walls
Where winter morning finds its perfect shelter,
Building sanctuaries of untouched stillness
Between weathered foundation stones that hold
Memories of all who've sought refuge here.

Behind ancient walls, protected spaces cradle
The remnants of autumn's abandoned gardens -
Dried stalks, scattered seeds, abandoned nests -
Each one held in morning's gentle embrace,
Finding shelter from December's wild winds.

The winter sun breaks through gathering clouds,
Blessing these sheltered and sacred spaces
Where small creatures seek their safety still
Among tumbled stones and twisted roots,
Peace dwelling deep in hidden corners.

Morning light reveals these quiet harbors
In our winter-transformed waiting world:
Hollow trees offering their ancient shelter,
Deep thickets and snow-capped stone walls,
Each one standing ready with sanctuary.

* * *

DAY 13: REFUGE

Afternoon

Winter afternoon illuminates with gentle grace
Ancient barns that stand their patient watch,
Their weathered boards glowing with memories
Of generations who have sought their shelter,
Finding peace within these trusted walls.

Centuries of stories rest in silent rafters,
Written in the deep-grained winter quiet,
While afternoon light streams unhindered
Through warped window frames, blessing
All these perfectly protected spaces.

The afternoon world grows smaller here,
Contained within these sheltering walls
Where dust motes dance through sunbeams
Like golden snow in perfect stillness,
Time slowing to a peaceful dream.

Here in darkness behind winter-worn doors,
Smoothed by countless seeking hands,
Peace dwells in shadows undisturbed,
Offering refuge from life's wild storms,
Shelter perfect in its simplicity.

* * *

DAY 13: REFUGE

Evening

Night approaches these sacred harbors now
Where lamplight spills through frosted windows,
Each glowing square becoming a beacon
That promises warmth and welcome still
Against the gathering winter darkness.

Evening draws us to bright hearth fires,
To circles of shared light and shelter
Where stories find their quiet voices,
Where peace spreads protective wings
Over all who gather in its keeping.

The moon silvers snow-crowned garden walls
Standing guard over sleep-quiet spaces,
While stars wheel their ancient paths,
Their faithful light offering refuge still
To every weary, seeking soul below.

Darkness brings its own kind of shelter,
Wrapping the world in velvet shadows
Where peace keeps its patient vigil,
Standing guard through longest night
Until morning returns with light.

* * *

DAY 13: REFUGE

"God is ... refuge and strength, a very present help in trouble."

Psalm 46:1

Reflections on the Day's Theme

_____

_____

_____

_____

_____

_____

_____

_____

_____

_____

_____

_____

* * *

DAY 13: REFUGE

Bridge to Tomorrow

Safe harbor beckons
Through winter storm and shadow
Peace waits at the door

Advent Insight

In medieval times, monasteries kept their doors open throughout Advent, offering refuge to travelers braving winter's darkest days. This practice mirrored the Christmas story itself, with the search for shelter becoming a sacred act of both giving and receiving peace.

Tomorrow's Call

Create a simple gesture of welcome for tomorrow—a light in the window, an open door, a chair turned in readiness. Let this preparation remind you that peace often becomes stronger when shared and that refuge can be both offered and accepted.

#

DAY 14: MOONLIT NIGHT

The moon is a friend for the lonesome to talk to.

—Carl Sandburg

The moon ascends, its light subdued,
A silver calm for hearts renewed.
In shadows soft, its glow brings peace,
A night of rest, a sweet release.

DAY 14: MOONLIT NIGHT

Morning

Dawn finds the winter moon still shining,
A pale ghost lingering in brightening skies,
Holding night's sacred secrets in its silver face
While sunrise paints the eastern horizon gold
With promises of transcendent morning light.

Frost sparkles on winter branches everywhere,
Where moonlight blessed the darkness hours,
Leaving behind its crystalline benediction
On this threshold between night and daybreak,
When two lights share the transforming sky.

Morning mist holds memories of moonlight still
In its pearlescent and mysterious depths, while
The moon's face grows gradually transparent,
Fading into winter-blue heavens above us,
Like a dream dissolving at gentle waking.

The world wears moon-blessed silence still,
Even as day claims its ascending throne.
Some magic from the night remains with us,
Caught in shadows and spider web patterns,
In drops of silver-touched morning dew.

* * *

DAY 14: MOONLIT NIGHT

Afternoon

Beyond the azure depths of winter afternoon,
The moon continues its eternal sacred journey,
Unseen but present, like peace sleeping deep
Beneath the surface of our busy passing hours,
Waiting patient for evening's unveiling.

Shadows hold themselves differently today,
When moon-tides pull at earthbound waters,
Though bright sun commands afternoon's light
With golden rays and stark-cast shade lines,
Nature knows night's queen approaches still.

Winter branches trace their dark patterns now
Against afternoon's crystal-perfect air,
Rehearsing for their evening collaboration
When moonlight will transform their shapes
Into silver-etched celestial sculptures.

The day holds its breath in anticipation,
Each moment drawing us ever closer
To night's radiant revelation, when
The moon will reclaim her rightful realm
From sun's gradually retreating rays.

* * *

DAY 14: MOONLIT NIGHT

Evening

The moon rises profound and perfectly full
Over our winter-transformed waiting world,
Transmuting mundane shadows to mystery,
Each darkened corner becoming sacred space
Under her ancient and resplendent blessing.

Silver light pours across untouched snow,
Creating seas of scattered starlight here
Where familiar fields lay only hours before,
While night opens its celestial flower,
Blessing earth with perfect lunar peace.

Shadows pool like India ink beneath trees
While moonlight silvers every reaching branch,
Creating spirit-forests in ordinary woods,
Night's transfiguration now complete
Under December's cold and perfect moon.

Our world inhales pure moonlight deeply,
Exhales waves of sacred winter silence
Across illuminated fields of snow, while
Peace flows from above in silver streams,
Bathing earth in ancient, endless light.

* * *

DAY 14: MOONLIT NIGHT

"When I look at your heavens, the work of your fingers, the moon and the stars, which you have set in place, what is man that you are mindful of him, and the son of man that you care for him?"

Psalm 8:3-4

Reflections on the Day's Theme

_____

_____

_____

_____

_____

_____

_____

_____

_____

* * *

DAY 14: MOONLIT NIGHT

Bridge to Tomorrow

Moon's silver path shines
Across dark December skies
Peace lights our way home

Advent Insight

In northern monastic communities, the December full moon—known as the "Oak Moon" or "Long Night's Moon"—held deep significance during Advent. Its silvery glow reminded us that even in winter's most prolonged darkness, a peaceful radiance endures to guide our way forward.

Tomorrow's Call

Before you sleep tonight, pay attention to where the moonlight touches your space—perhaps through a window or in the gleam of snow outside. Remember this spot, and tomorrow, let it remind you that peace often arrives like moonlight—gentle, constant, and able to transform darkness.

# # #

Joy

Joy rises bright, a song takes flight,
Its rhythm strong, its glow alight.
Within our hearts, it finds its place,
A radiant gift, a warm embrace.

Celebration

Joy

Joy bursts forth like golden light on a winter's day, warming the heart and illuminating the world. The deep gladness comes from knowing we are loved and cherished, not for what we do but simply for who we are. Advent invites us to celebrate this unshakable joy.

In a season of preparation, joy reminds us to pause and rejoice. It is found in grand moments of celebration and in small, everyday blessings—a shared laugh, a kind word, a moment of stillness. Joy is infectious, lifting us and those around us.

This week, we explore the many faces of joy. Through verse and reflection, may you find joy that brightens your days and lights the way for others. Let it flow freely, filling your heart and home with warmth.

Begin this week's journey of joy...

DAY 15: LAUGHTER

Laughter is the sun that drives winter from the human face.

—Victor Hugo

The sound of joy, a gentle ring,
Like laughter bright, it starts to sing.
It echoes far, a cheerful song,
A gift of love to carry along.

DAY 15: LAUGHTER

Morning

Sunrise catches ice crystals in joyful dance,
Setting the entire winter world aglitter with delight
While sparrows hop and chatter through branches,
Their small joy bubbling through morning stillness
Like children's laughter echoing through clear air.

Morning frost draws whimsical patterns on windows,
Creating fairy landscapes and crystalline gardens
That sparkle with improbable, delightful designs,
While even bare branches seem to smile upward,
Ice-jeweled and radiant in the climbing sun.

The day awakens with unexpected playfulness,
Finding humor in steam-dragon morning breath,
In rabbit tracks that wander without purpose,
In squirrels playing endless chase through snow,
Nature's own comedy unfolding in winter light.

Wind chimes ring their bright, random music,
A melody of pure, spontaneous celebration
That sets the morning world gently dancing,
Joy ringing clear through winter stillness now,
Breaking solemnity with songs of gladness.

* * *

DAY 15: LAUGHTER

Afternoon

Winter sunlight plays eternal hide-and-seek
Through racing clouds that spill their bounty,
Scattering snowflake confetti with abandon
Across an afternoon's bright playground where
Even ancient trees dance with passing wind.

Chickadees bounce between laden branches,
Their dee-dee-dee songs a running winter joke
Through the transformed December landscape,
While sunbeams catch tumbling snowflakes
Turning endless cartwheels through bright air.

Ice cracks its scattered applause suddenly
Across thawing afternoon puddles of light
Where sky reflects in countless fragments,
Breaking endless blue into kaleidoscopes
Of tumbled, unexpected winter beauty.

The world spins afternoon tales of delight,
Finding joy in life's simplest offerings:
Snow sliding from overburdened branches,
Sun breaking through storm clouds sudden,
Nature's happiness bubbling ever upward.

* * *

DAY 15: LAUGHTER

Evening

Stars emerge with unmistakable mischief now,
Scattering their ancient light across dark skies
Like diamonds tossed by celestial jesters
Over winter evening's velvet-perfect darkness,
Each point of light a spark of cosmic joy.

The moon rolls its luminous face upward,
Above horizon's edge, telling age-old jokes
To listening trees whose shadows dance
Across fresh-fallen snow in silent delight,
Playing endless games with winter night.

Evening light plays its gentle hide-and-seek,
Turning cosmic darkness into wonderland
Where joy scatters rainbow laughter still
Across twilight's deepening canvas of night,
Each moment sparking new celebration.

Night arrives wearing joy's gentle blessing,
Wrapping our world in star-shine promise
And infinite possibilities for dreaming,
While happiness settles softly downward
Like benediction from the winter stars.

* * *

DAY 15: LAUGHTER

"A joyful heart is good medicine, but a crushed spirit dries up the bones."

Proverbs 17:22

Reflections on the Day's Theme

* * *

DAY 15: LAUGHTER

Bridge to Tomorrow

Winter sunlight dances
Through frost-touched morning windows
Joy breaks like dawn's smile

Advent Insight

Medieval mystery plays performed during Advent often included moments of holy humor, reflecting the belief that joy and laughter are sacred gifts. The tradition of "Holy Innocents' Day," honoring the youngest among us, highlighted the divine delight in children's laughter, reminding us that joy often appears unbidden in moments of pure and simple delight.

Tomorrow's Call

Put something that brings you joy—a photograph, a child's drawing, a memento from a happy moment—where tomorrow's light will reach it first. Let it remind you that laughter, like joy, is meant to be both unexpected and shared.

# # #

DAY 16: MUSIC

Where words fail, music speaks.

—Hans Christian Andersen

The world takes flight on wings of song,
Its melody pure, deep and strong.
In every note, the soul takes part,
A symphony that gladly lifts the heart.

DAY 16: MUSIC

Morning

First light orchestrates its winter symphony,
Setting crystalline morning air vibrating
With harmonies of frost and filtered sunlight
As frozen droplets shatter into rainbows
And birds begin tuning their bright instruments.

Morning bells ring their bronze voices outward
Across snow-hushed winter landscapes where
Even profound silence carries its own music,
Each moment adding notes to dawn's score,
Building toward day's complete composition.

The wind conducts bare branches masterfully,
Creating winter's unexpected symphony
Where every twig and stem contributes
Its particular note to nature's endless song,
Morning's orchestra playing heaven's music.

Sunlight strikes the ice-touched world anew,
Creating glass-chime songs from frozen drops,
While the day begins its grand performance,
Joy rising with each perfectly placed note
Through winter morning's cathedral air.

* * *

DAY 16: MUSIC

Afternoon

Winter trees play their ancient wind songs now,
Branches swaying to rhythms old as heartbeats,
Moving together in December afternoon light,
Creating endless concerts of shadow and gleam
For those who pause long enough to listen.

Water music flows beneath transparent ice,
Stream songs continuing their patient way
Through winter's temporary transformations,
While overhead, geese trumpets echo still
Through endless fields of afternoon blue.

The bright world resonates with countless voices:
Pine needles whisper their gentle harmony,
Snow adds its squeaking percussion notes,
Nature's endless orchestra playing still
Through winter afternoon's perfect hours.

Sound waves ripple outward through clear air,
Each note finding its appointed place and time
In the grand composition of December day,
While joy flows through every measure played
In afternoon's continuing celebration.

* * *

DAY 16: MUSIC

Evening

Night approaches with string-song gentleness,
Stars taking their places like musicians ready
In winter evening's expanding concert hall,
Each point of light preparing to perform
Heaven's ancient and endless evening score.

The moon raises its conductor's bright baton
Over twilight's gathering orchestra below,
Directing stellar harmonies that spiral down
Through layers of darkness toward earth,
Blessing all who listen to night's music.

Evening wind carries remembered melodies
From day's completed symphony of sound:
Bird song, branch song, bell song blending
In the gathering darkness of December night
To create winter evening's perfect concert.

The world settles into its rhythmic peace,
Finding joy in darkness where music flows
Never ceasing but changing instruments,
As stars begin their celestial songs anew,
Night's symphony reaching completion.

* * *

DAY 16: MUSIC

"Addressing one another in psalms and hymns and spiritual songs, ... making melody to the LORD with your heart."

Ephesians 5:19

Reflections on the Day's Theme

_____

_____

_____

_____

_____

_____

_____

_____

_____

_____

_____

_____

* * *

DAY 16: MUSIC

Bridge to Tomorrow

Carols fill the air
Notes rise like winter sparrows
Joy takes wing and soars

Advent Insight

The tradition of Advent carols did not begin in grand churches but in village streets, where medieval singers known as "waits" traveled from house to house, sharing songs of hope and joy. These carolers believed that music had the power to open hearts and build bridges between neighbors, bringing light and warmth to the darkest days of the year, one doorstep at a time.

Tomorrow's Call

Choose a melody—perhaps a favorite carol or simple tune—that you'll carry into tomorrow. Let it be your companion through the day, reminding you that music grows stronger when shared with others.

# # #

DAY 17: DANCE

Dance is the hidden language of the soul.

—Martha Graham

The rhythm stirs, the heart takes flight,
Each step a spark, a pure delight.
In every move, the spirit sings,
A joy that only dancing brings.

DAY 17: DANCE

Morning

Snowflakes begin their intricate morning ballet,
Twirling gracefully through brightening winter air
In perfectly choreographed, crystalline descent,
Each flake following its appointed ancient steps
Across nature's vast December performance stage.

The warming wind leads bare branches gently
In their slow-motion morning ballet performance,
Moving now to rhythms felt rather than heard,
While winter birds wheel through empty spaces,
Creating aerial dances against brightening sky.

Sunbeams partner shadows in endless waltzes
Across newly fallen fields of untouched snow,
Creating intricate patterns of light and darkness
That shift with each passing winter cloud above,
Nature's own sacred dance of day beginning.

Morning mist rises from frozen ground below,
Each curl and spiral moving with deliberate grace,
Perfect as a dancer's practiced morning gesture,
Joy expressed in movement pure and flowing,
As the day's bright dance unfolds before us.

* * *

DAY 17: DANCE

Afternoon

Winter light spins through crystalline prisms,
Scattering rainbow dancers across snow banks
Where wind-lifted ice crystals perform still
Their endless and ethereal winter waltz,
Each moment a new choreography of joy.

Dried leaves still clinging to winter branches
Dance their afternoon gavotte in golden light,
Each movement a celebration of persistence,
Of finding joy in winter's transformation,
Of dancing through December's bright hours.

The passing day whirls toward evening now
In carefully practiced and perfect winter steps,
Cloud shadows racing across fields of snow
While trees bow and sway in partnered grace,
Each element joining earth's endless dance.

Even the stillest afternoon holds motion,
Ice shifting on pond surfaces below us,
Steam rising from sun-warmed earth still,
The world in constant choreography,
Dancing through each precious moment.

* * *

DAY 17: DANCE

Evening

Stars begin their nightly celestial pavane
Across heaven's vast ballroom floor above,
While northern lights rehearse their flowing
Choreography across winter's dark stage,
Nature's greatest dancers taking their places.

Night air holds suspended motion perfect,
In its crystalline and mysterious depths,
Where moonbeams partner shadow dancers
In their age-old and eternal performance
Across fresh-fallen fields of virgin snow.

The evening world turns in stately measure,
Following cosmic rhythms beyond time,
That move both stars and mortal souls
In their eternal circular performances,
Joy spinning through infinite space.

Darkness brings its own graceful dancers:
Silent owls gliding on velvet wing beats,
Fox tracks writing their delicate patterns,
While overhead, stars continue wheeling
In their perfectly endless winter ballet.

* * *

DAY 17: DANCE

"Let them praise his name with dancing, making melody to
him with tambourine and lyre!"

Psalm 149:3

Reflections on the Day's Theme

* * *

DAY 17: DANCE

Bridge to Tomorrow

Snowflakes waltz midair
Winter writes its flowing dance
Joy moves without sound

Advent Insight

In some European Christian traditions, especially in France and Spain, sacred dance was integral to Advent celebrations. Known as the "dance of waiting," it began with measured, contemplative steps and grew more exuberant as Christmas drew near. This practice reflected the belief that there is room for joyful and graceful celebration even in the stillness of waiting.

Tomorrow's Call

Notice something in constant motion—perhaps a branch in the wind, clouds across the sky, or your own breathing. Let this natural choreography remind you tomorrow that joy often expresses itself in movement, whether seen or unseen.

#

DAY 18: GOLDEN LIGHT

Light tomorrow with today.

—Elizabeth Barrett Browning

The golden rays of dawn's embrace,
A touch of warmth, a beam of grace.
They brighten paths and lift the soul,
A joy that makes the broken whole.

DAY 18: GOLDEN LIGHT

Morning

First light breaks across the horizon in amber waves,
Transforming this ordinary December morning world
Into an illuminated manuscript written in pure gold,
Each moment a celebration of radiance unfolding,
Nature's alchemy turning winter darkness to treasure.

Each frost crystal becomes a prism of celebration,
Scattering sunrise colors through brightening air
While dawn paints the world in precious metals,
Setting every snowdrift alight with golden fire,
Joy sparking from each transformed surface.

The day arrives wearing its crown of morning glory,
Touching bare branches with transcendent light
Until each twig and stem blazes with inner fire,
Nature's own alchemy transforming winter dawn
Into a celebration of precious golden moments.

Winter sunrise pours its treasure across snow fields
Where every crystal catches and multiplies light,
Creating seas of scattered gold beneath our feet,
While joy rises with the strengthening morning sun,
Each ray a blessing in winter's brightening kingdom.

* * *

DAY 18: GOLDEN LIGHT

Afternoon

December sun reaches its full radiant strength,
Turning winter afternoon into treasury of light
Where even shadows wear edges of burnished gold,
Each moment precious beyond mortal counting
In this transformed and transcendent landscape.

Sunlight spills between clouds in bright columns,
Heaven's spotlights illuminating random patches
Of ordinary earth with extraordinary radiance,
Creating sacred spaces in afternoon shadows
Where joy pools like liquid gold beneath trees.

The world bathes in these amber-perfect hours,
Each passing moment transformed to precious metal,
Time itself becoming a river of pure golden light
Flowing across the winter-transformed landscape,
Every instant a celebration of celestial alchemy.

Air holds suspended gold in slanting rays,
Visible in bright beams through bare branches
Where dust motes dance their eternal patterns,
Each particle carrying its own small radiance,
Adding to afternoon's accumulated treasure.

* * *

DAY 18: GOLDEN LIGHT

Evening

The sun spends its last gold coins lavishly,
Scattering wealth across darkening horizon
In one final celebration of passing day,
While clouds catch and hold reflected glory
Like winter evening's farewell performance.

Light changes currency as daylight fades,
From bright gold to deeper amber tones,
Each moment growing somehow richer still
As day's treasure gradually transforms itself
Into evening's more subtle inheritance.

The world holds golden memory in silence:
In snow-reflected sunset's final moments,
In ice-caught amber light growing dimmer,
In windows wearing glory's last remnants
Against the approaching winter night.

Last rays paint winter trees in precious metal,
Each branch becoming an arrow of pure gold
Pointing toward the first emerging stars above,
While joy lingers in these transitional moments
As night's own treasures prepare to emerge.

* * *

DAY 18: GOLDEN LIGHT

"The light shines in the darkness, and the darkness has not overcome it."

John 1:5

Reflections on the Day's Theme

* * *

DAY 18: GOLDEN LIGHT

Bridge to Tomorrow

Sun pours liquid gold
Through winter's crystal morning
Joy flows bright and warm

Advent Insight

During the Middle Ages, churches prepared for Christmas by polishing their sacred vessels and gilded ornaments, ensuring they would gleam in Advent's slanting winter light. This tradition reminded the faithful that joy, like golden light, has the power to illuminate and transform even the simplest moments into reflections of divine glory.

Tomorrow's Call

Find a spot where tomorrow's sunlight will create a special moment, such as touching a window or catching a metal surface. Mark this space in your mind, and let it remind you that joy often comes in gleaming moments that transform the everyday into the extraordinary.

# # #

DAY 19: SHARED FEAST

The best moments are shared over a table.

—Unknown

Around the table, hearts unite,
In simple bread, a shared delight.
Each hand that gives, each one that takes,
A joy-filled bond that never breaks.

DAY 19: SHARED FEAST

Morning

The kitchen wakes before this winter morning sun,
Breathing warmth and aromatic promise into darkness
While bowls stand ready like open expectations,
Measuring cups await morning's bright alchemy,
And recipes unfold their dog-eared family wisdom.

Steam rises from fresh coffee into frost-touched air
As morning light spills across waiting countertops,
Finding cookie cutters, rolling pins, bread rising
Under careful cloths, each preparation becoming
A prayer of thanksgiving for those who'll gather here.

Our house fills with breakfast's welcome aromas -
Cinnamon, vanilla, fresh bread transforming air -
Each scent a herald of coming celebration,
While winter birds gather at feeders outside,
All creatures sharing morning's abundant feast.

Sunlight pours through kitchen windows generously,
Blessing cutting boards and well-worn cooking pots,
Everything ready for hands that will craft today's
Offerings of love made visible in shared food,
Joy rising like warm bread in winter morning light.

* * *

DAY 19: SHARED FEAST

Afternoon

Preparations transform ordinary afternoon hours
Into occasions of shared anticipation and delight,
While ovens warm the gathering winter air
And countertops overflow with promised feasts,
Each moment drawing us toward evening's sharing.

December sunlight touches serving bowls with grace,
Illuminating generations of handed-down recipes
Written in fading ink and careful cursive script,
Each ingredient measured in memory and love,
Each dish holding stories of feasts remembered.

The afternoon fills with peaceful, joyful industry,
Chopping boards keeping rhythm with quiet talk,
While tasting spoons test seasoning with care,
Tomorrow's bread taking shape from ancient knowledge
Of flour and water, time and temperature.

Stories circle through the busy working kitchen
Like herbs crushed to release their essence,
Each tale flavoring this gathering December day
While outside, snow begins its gentle descent,
Nature offering its own feast for hungry eyes.

* * *

DAY 19: SHARED FEAST

Evening

Night arrives bearing stars like scattered salt
Across heaven's dark tablecloth, while inside
Candles flicker on carefully set tables where
Crystal catches light like imprisoned stars,
Each place setting a promise of welcome joy.

Steam rises from shared dishes into evening air
Rich with conversation's gentle music flowing,
While outside, winter presses against windows,
Making this warm circle more precious still,
This gathering more blessed by stark contrast.

Faces glow in candlelight and fellowship now,
Each smile part of evening's abundant feast,
Every voice adding its particular seasoning
To the rich stew of friendship and family
Simmering in December's deep cooking pot.

Time slows its hurried pace to savor fully
This circle of light and shared companionship
Where simple food becomes pure sacrament,
Ordinary moments transform to precious memory,
And joy spreads like butter on warm bread.

* * *

DAY 19: SHARED FEAST

"They broke bread in their homes and ate together with glad and sincere hearts."

Acts 2:46

Reflections on the Day's Theme

* * *

DAY 19: SHARED FEAST

Bridge to Tomorrow

Breaking bread with love
Stories shared like winter wine
Joy fills every cup

Advent Insight

In ancient Christian tradition, "love feasts" during Advent brought communities together to share simple meals. These agape gatherings were characterized by shared food, songs, and stories, celebrating the belief that joy is multiplied by breaking bread together, even in the humblest of circumstances.

Tomorrow's Call

Set a place at your table tonight for tomorrow's meal—perhaps with a special plate or napkin, a sprig of evergreen, or a small candle. Let this preparation remind you that joy flourishes when we intentionally create space to share it with others.

# # #

Day 20: Festive Spirit

Joy is the simplest form of gratitude.

—Karl Barth

The air is bright with festive cheer,
A time of joy with Christmas near.
With hearts aglow, the world takes part,
In pleasure that springs from every heart.

DAY 20: FESTIVE SPIRIT

Morning

Morning arrives wearing its celebration robes,
Each windowpane decorated with frost's artistry,
While winter birds sing their joyful carols loud
Through snow-laden branches reaching skyward,
Every moment a gift of December delight.

Winter sunrise scatters diamond light abundantly
Across fresh-fallen snow, magically transforming
Ordinary morning into pure celebration where
Even bare trees wear their reaching branches
Like dancers dressed for nature's winter ball.

The day awakens to infinite possibility now,
Each precious moment wrapped in bright promise,
Every hour a gift waiting to be opened slowly
As December sunlight spills across pure snow
In streams of pure and perfect celebration.

Anticipation rings through brightening air
Like distant bells across frozen winter fields,
While the climbing sun blesses this ordinary
Tuesday morning with extraordinary light,
Making sacred space of winter's dawning.

* * *

DAY 20: FESTIVE SPIRIT

Afternoon

The transformed world wears festive colors proudly:
Cardinal-red feathers against evergreen branches,
Holly berries bright beside silver-dusted snow,
While winter shadows paint their purple patterns
Across the celebrating December afternoon.

Children's laughter carries through crystal air
Where snowmen stand like welcome party guests,
Their coal smiles and carrot noses proclaiming
Joy in nature's gift of fresh-fallen snow,
Each moment a celebration of winter wonder.

Each passing hour sparkles with bright occasion,
Ordinary errands transformed by December joy
Into something unexpectedly rich and strange,
Where even grocery store journeys become
Pilgrimages of pure winter delight.

Time dances through these brightening hours
To music heard in quickening heartbeats,
While winter light plays through parting clouds,
Creating spotlights for Earth's performance
Of afternoon's continuing celebration.

* * *

DAY 20: FESTIVE SPIRIT

Evening

Night arrives dressed in her finest winter garments:
Stars scattered like sequins across heaven's dark
Velvet, while below, windows spark golden welcome
Through December's early-gathering darkness,
Each light a declaration of festive spirit.

The evening world shimmers with countless lights
Strung through trees like earth-bound constellations,
Each glowing point becoming a bright declaration
That darkness cannot claim these sacred hours
Where joy maintains its celebratory vigil.

Candlelight spills across December tables
Where friendship shares its gathered treasures,
While outside, winter evening deepens gently
Into pools of sacred darkness held between
Islands of continuing celebration.

Time flows like music through the gathering night,
Each moment a note in winter's joyful song
Of starlight, lamplight, blessed candlelight,
All blending in the deepening darkness
To light our hearts toward morning's dawn.

* * *

DAY 20: FESTIVE SPIRIT

"Then he said to them, 'Go your way. Eat the fat and drink sweet wine and send portions to anyone who has nothing ready, for this day is holy to our LORD. And do not be grieved, for the joy of the LORD is your strength.'"

Nehemiah 8:10

Reflections on the Day's Theme

_____

_____

_____

_____

_____

_____

_____

* * *

DAY 20: FESTIVE SPIRIT

Bridge to Tomorrow

Bells ring through the air
Winter skies fill with their song
Joy calls out to joy

Advent Insight

During the Advent season of yesteryear, bell ringers crafted special "joy peals" for the third week, celebrated as Gaudete (Rejoice) Sunday. These distinctive patterns of ringing became increasingly more elaborate as Christmas drew near, creating a rising tide of joy and inviting all who heard them to join in the spirit of celebration.

Tomorrow's Call

Choose something representing celebration to you, such as a bell, a ribbon, or a meaningful ornament. Place it where you'll encounter it tomorrow, letting it remind you that joy often arrives as an invitation, asking us to join its ongoing celebration.

# # #

DAY 21: STARRY SKIES

Though my soul may set in darkness, it will rise in perfect light; I have loved the stars too fondly to be fearful of the night.

—Sarah Williams

The stars align, their light unfolds,
A canvas vast of tales retold.
In every spark, the heavens show,
A joy that guides and bids us grow.

DAY 21: STARRY SKIES

Morning

The last stars shimmer through breaking dawn,
Orion's belt loosening as night retreats,
While the Pleiades dance their final measures
Before surrendering to morning's advance,
Each constellation bidding day welcome.

Heaven's map gradually folds its legends,
Star paths dissolving in brightening blue,
Yet their cosmic dance continues unseen,
Teaching us how joy persists through changes,
Through every transition darkness to light.

Frost holds echoes of starlight in crystal,
Each prism remembering night's bright gems
While sunrise claims the eastern horizon,
Transferring heaven's light from stars to sun,
One celestial glory yielding to another.

Morning birds begin their dawn chorus now
Where stars once sang their silent songs,
Day's musicians replacing night's dancers
As Earth turns its face from stellar maps
Toward our nearest star's approaching light.

* * *

DAY 21: STARRY SKIES

Afternoon

Star patterns wheel unseen above our heads
Through flickering December afternoon sky,
Their ancient stories flowing on silent,
Moving to rhythms older than memory
While we live our brief daylight hours.

Somewhere far beyond this cerulean dome,
Celestial fires burn without ceasing,
Teaching us through their constant presence
That distance cannot diminish brightness,
That joy endures beyond our seeing.

Each snowflake catches winter sunlight,
Reflecting stellar patterns in miniature,
As if heaven has scattered tiny mirrors
Across Earth's white December canvas,
Each crystal a map of cosmic design.

Afternoon light travels vast distances,
Our own star sending messages of joy
Through space that holds countless others,
Reminding us we're part of something
Greater than our small certainties.

* * *

DAY 21: STARRY SKIES

Evening

First stars pierce December's velvet dusk,
Polaris claiming its constant northern watch
While stellar sentinels take evening posts,
Each one awakening in appointed time
To join night's grand processional.

Cassiopeia raises her royal throne
High above northern winter forests,
While Great Bear prowls horizon's edge,
All following ancient star paths scripted
Before Earth knew human wonderment.

The Milky Way unfurls its cosmic ribbon,
Spilling stellar jewels across night sky,
Each point of light a burning story,
A celebration of celestial fire
Dancing through infinite darkness.

Heaven's constellations wheel in glory,
Teaching earthbound hearts to look up,
To find joy in patterns beyond reach,
To read stories written in starlight
Across December's darkening dome.

* * *

DAY 21: STARRY SKIES

"The heavens declare the glory of God, and the sky above proclaims his handiwork."

Psalm 19:1

Reflections on the Day's Theme

* * *

DAY 21: STARRY SKIES

Bridge to Tomorrow

Night stars dance above
Each point a singing light now
Joy spans Earth and sky

Advent Insight

In the quiet depths of Advent's longest nights, medieval monks in monastery towers charted the stars, marveling at the "celestial symphony of joy" they believed filled the heavens. For them, the stars' endless dance across the sky was a lesson in how to celebrate life—with both awe and harmony, guided by divine order.

Tomorrow's Call

Before you sleep tonight, find a star to call your own—whether visible through a window or imagined in your mind's eye. Let its eternal light bridge your today and tomorrow, reminding you that joy, like starlight, travels across vast distances to touch us exactly when we need it.

# # #

Love

A quiet flame, a tender glow,
The truest gift we'll ever know.
Love speaks in acts both small and great,
A bond of hearts, a joyful fate.

Connection

Love

Love is at the heart of Advent and Christmas. It is the gift that transcends time and space, uniting us in ways words cannot fully express. Love is the light that warms, the bond that unites, and the force that heals. It invites us into a relationship with God and one another, calling us to reflect that same love in our actions.

This week, we reflect on love's power to transform and restore. Love is felt in grand gestures and quiet, everyday acts of kindness and care. It is a flame that burns brightly even in the coldest seasons, reminding us of the warmth of connection and the depth of grace.

During these final days of Advent, let us carry Christ's love in our hearts and into the world. May this love inspire us to embrace others with compassion, heal with forgiveness, and shine brightly as reflections of divine love.

Begin this week's journey of love...

DAY 22: FAMILY

In every conceivable manner, the family is a link to our past, bridge to our future.

—Alex Haley

Within the home, where love abides,
The heart is filled, the world subsides.
A bond of trust, a gift sublime,
The connection grows with passing time.

DAY 22: FAMILY

Morning

Footsteps creak familiar paths down morning stairs,
Each sound a cherished voice in home's symphony,
While coffee scents the gradually warming air,
And love speaks through all our simple gestures,
The quiet rituals of family awakening.

Kitchen light spills across our well-worn table
Where generations have gathered through years,
Their stories etched in wood grain patterns,
In handed-down china's careful arrangements,
In recipes marked with beloved marble notes.

Outside, winter presses against frosted windows
While inside, morning rituals unfold with grace:
Toast browning, tea steeping, bacon sizzling,
Each action a thread in family's precious fabric,
Weaving moments into lifelong memories.

The house holds its collected warmth close,
Sheltering sleep-tousled children's laughter,
Morning-quiet parents, visiting relatives,
All bound in love's familiar rhythms here,
Where belonging needs no explanation.

* * *

DAY 22: FAMILY

Afternoon

Winter sunlight warms treasured photographs
Where younger versions of ourselves still smile,
Each frame holding stories of summers past,
Of christenings, graduations, weddings shared,
Love's history captured in golden afternoon light.

The day fills with gentle familiar motion:
Cards dealt at kitchen tables worn smooth,
Children sprawled with books or endless games,
Someone napping in grandfather's favorite chair,
Each moment precious in its ordinary grace.

Time moves differently within these walls
Where memories layer like gentle winter snow,
Building landscapes of deepest belonging
That weather every storm and passing season,
Growing richer with each gathering year.

Shadows lengthen across cherished carpets
Where generations have walked before us,
Their footsteps echoing still in hallways,
In creaking stairs, in beloved corners
Where love has made its dwelling place.

* * *

DAY 22: FAMILY

Evening

Night draws our family circle closer still,
Gathering everyone in pools of lamplight
Where stories flow like warm honey shared,
Sweet with remembering, rich with wisdom
Accumulated through years of loving.

Ancient tales find their newest listeners,
While fresh chapters unfold in tonight's
Gentle conversations around the fire,
Each voice adding its particular music
To our family's continuing story.

Evening deepens into profound comfort
Around tables bright with beloved faces,
Some present only in treasured memory,
Yet still part of this unbroken circle
Where love transcends time's boundaries.

Together we hold this sacred space now
Against winter darkness gathering deep,
Creating warmth that will remain with us
Long after we part, carried in our hearts
Like embers from the family hearth.

* * *

DAY 22: FAMILY

"... how good and pleasant it is when brothers dwell in unity!"

Psalm 133:1

Reflections on the Day's Theme

_____

_____

_____

_____

_____

_____

_____

_____

_____

_____

_____

_____

_____

_____

_____

* * *

DAY 22: FAMILY

Bridge to Tomorrow

Hearts gather like stars
Around home's warming hearth light
Love builds bridges here

Advent Insight

The "Advent hearth" tradition brought families together in northern European homes as they kept their fire burning through the season's longest nights. Each member took turns tending the flame, a ritual symbolizing how love, like firelight, thrives when nurtured by many hands and hearts.

Tomorrow's Call

Write down the names of everyone who has helped tend your heart's flame—both family by blood and those chosen. Keep this list where tomorrow's light can find it, and let each name inspire a small act of connection as the day unfolds.

# # #

DAY 23: WARM EMBRACE

A hug is a silent way of saying you matter to me.

—Unknown

A hug that holds, a hand that stays,
A warmth that brightens weary days.
In every act of care and grace,
A love eternal takes its place.

DAY 23: WARM EMBRACE

Morning

The sun reaches gentle arms across the horizon,
Gathering darkness into morning's first light,
While winter dawn embraces the sleeping world
In gradual warmth that touches frozen earth
With tenderness born of ancient knowing.

Frost retreats beneath love's patient warming,
As morning light wraps bare branches gently
In understanding born of countless dawns,
Teaching us again how warmth returns always
To embrace what winter's night left frozen.

Steam rises from morning cups like shared breath,
Warming hands that circle ceramic hearts,
While winter birds huddle close on branches,
Sharing heat and crumbs and precious space,
Teaching lessons of togetherness and care.

Our house holds its gathered warmth within
Like a mother cradling her cherished child,
Each room becoming shelter and embrace,
Where morning light pours benediction
Through windows wearing frost's lace patterns.

* * *

DAY 23: WARM EMBRACE

Afternoon

December sunlight fills empty spaces perfectly
Between bare trees with golden loving presence,
Wrapping winter-quiet gardens in gentle light
That remembers summer's nurturing warmth,
That promises spring's inevitable returning.

The afternoon world draws close around us,
Gathering shadows like protective blankets
Around winter-chilled corners of the day,
While sunlight embraces every living thing
In arms of patient, enduring radiance.

Warmth pools in sheltered, protected places
Where bitter wind cannot scatter comfort,
Where small creatures find their refuge still,
Where afternoon light lingers longest now,
Teaching us love's patient, gentle ways.

Time flows like honey through quiet hours
While winter light embraces sleeping earth,
Holding each moment precious and complete,
Each breath becoming soft reminder how
Love warms the coldest spaces within us.

* * *

DAY 23: WARM EMBRACE

Evening

Night approaches with velvet-gentle hands,
Gathering day's scattered, precious moments
Into darkness soft as love's forgiveness,
While stars emerge to hold our world close
In their ancient, infinite embrace above.

The evening air wraps close around houses
Now bright with welcoming window light,
Where families gather in circles of warmth,
Each room becoming a heart of brightness
Beating strong against winter darkness.

Hearth fires cradle these evening hours
In hands of flickering, nurturing light,
While outside, darkness deepens gently
Into pools of quiet comfort between
Our islands of warmth and belonging.

We learn from night's perfect example
How to hold each other through darkness,
Through light and all between seasons,
How love creates safe harbors still
In midst of winter's longest nights.

* * *

DAY 23: WARM EMBRACE

"Above all, keep loving one another earnestly, since love covers a multitude of sins."

1 Peter 4:8

Reflections on the Day's Theme

_____

_____

_____

_____

_____

_____

_____

_____

_____

_____

_____

_____

* * *

DAY 23: WARM EMBRACE

Bridge to Tomorrow

Arms open like dawn
Drawing night into morning
Love welcomes us home

Advent Insight

In monastic traditions, the "ritual of embrace" marked each evening of late Advent, as monks shared peace through a holy embrace before compline prayers. This practice reminded them that divine love often comes to us through human touch, and that every genuine embrace echoes the way God holds the world.

Tomorrow's Call

At day's end tonight, wrap your arms around yourself in a gentle embrace. Tomorrow, let this memory remind you to notice all the ways love reaches toward you—in a friend's smile, a kind word, a moment of grace—and be ready to extend that embrace to others.

# # #

DAY 24: SELFLESS GIFT

It's not how much we give, but with how much love.

—Adapted from Saint Teresa of Calcutta (Mother Teresa)

A gift not wrapped, nor tied with bow,
But love in action starts to show.
Its quiet deeds, its tender care,
A selfless gift, a love laid bare.

DAY 24: SELFLESS GIFT

Morning

Dawn arrives bearing morning's first light,
Offering its radiance without reservation
To every darkened corner of winter's world,
Each ray becoming a lesson in pure giving
Without thought or need of any return.

Winter birds scatter morning seeds generously,
Their small gifts spread across fresh-fallen snow
Where delicate tracks tell stories of night visitors,
Each creature leaving its own particular present
Of presence on this December morning stage.

The sun pours golden grace through bare branches
Like love streaming down from measureless heights,
Touching frozen earth with unconditional warmth
That asks nothing in this or any season,
That gives without counting or condition.

Morning frost releases countless diamonds,
Scattering across every waiting surface,
Teaching us how nature shares abundance,
Her beauty offered without reservation,
Her treasures given freely without price.

* * *

DAY 24: SELFLESS GIFT

Afternoon

December sunlight spends itself fully
Across the winter-transformed landscape now,
Each beam becoming precious offering given
Wholly to this present perfect moment,
Asking nothing in its pure returning.

Snow releases its gathered light generously
Into the deepening afternoon shadows,
While clouds part like curtains drawing back
To show heaven's endless gifts of blue,
Each moment a celebration of giving.

Time opens its generous hands completely,
Offering moments like wrapped presents
Adorned with winter's own pure wonder,
Each hour becoming celebration of love
That flows outward without ceasing.

The world turns toward evening gently,
In gestures of perfect completion now,
Where afternoon light demonstrates still
How to pour ourselves out utterly
Until nothing remains ungiven or held.

* * *

DAY 24: SELFLESS GIFT

Evening

Stars emerge bearing ancient light
That has traveled countless years through space
To touch our upturned wondering faces
With messages from distant burning suns,
Each beam a selfless journey completed.

Night spreads its velvet darkness around
Like a cloak wrapped around Earth's shoulders,
While moonlight shares its silvered grace
With every shadow-touched corner still,
Holding nothing back in reservation.

Windows bloom with welcoming golden warmth,
Spilling light across evening's fresh snow
In welcome to any passing wanderer,
Each home becoming burning heart of love
Offering shelter without condition.

The day releases its final precious gifts
Into approaching December darkness,
Teaching us love's deepest pure truth:
That everything we have is meant for giving,
To be shared in joy without measure.

* * *

DAY 24: SELFLESS GIFT

"For God so loved the world, that he gave his only Son, that whoever believes in him should not perish but have eternal life."

John 3:16

Reflections on the Day's Theme

* * *

DAY 24: SELFLESS GIFT

Bridge to Tomorrow

Love gives all it has
Like snow covering bare earth
Grace falls soft and deep

Advent Insight

The "hidden gift" tradition began in convents, where nuns would secretly leave small tokens of kindness for one another—a sprig of evergreen, a copied psalm, or a piece of fruit. These anonymous acts of giving taught that love's greatest joy often lies in giving freely, without expectation of recognition.

Tomorrow's Call

Choose something small yet meaningful to share as Christmas dawns. Let this preparation open your heart to the subtle ways love flows through the world, touching lives without any fanfare or announcement.

# # #

Christmas

A light is born, the world made new,
A star above, a promise true.
The dawn of hope, the birth of grace,
Love eternal, shining face to face.

Fulfillment

Christmas

Christmas is the fulfillment of the Advent journey, when light breaks through the darkness and love is born into the world. It is a time of rejoicing, celebrating the gift of Christ's presence among us, and reflecting on the profound beauty of hope fulfilled.

The light of Christmas reminds us that every step of the journey—through hope, peace, joy, and love—has prepared us for this moment. It invites us to open our hearts fully, embracing the wonder and grace of this holy day.

As you celebrate, may the light of Christmas shine brightly in your life. Let it fill your heart with peace and your days with joy, and may the love of Christ inspire you to carry this light into the world.

Begin today's journey of fulfillment...

BIRTH OF LIGHT

The only blind person at Christmastime is he who has not Christmas in his heart.

—Helen Keller

The world rejoices, dawn now breaks,
A child is born, the earth awakes.
With hope fulfilled and hearts set free,
Love's greatest gift, eternity.

BIRTH OF LIGHT

Morning

First light breaks across Christmas morning skies,
Heaven touching Earth with transcendent grace
As dawn arrives bearing its ancient promise,
Each ray remembering that first sacred morning
When Light itself was born anew for all.

The world wakes to complete transformation,
Every shadow yielding to radiant blessing
That pours through winter darkness like love
Streaming down from heaven's highest place,
Like eternal hope made manifest in light.

Morning frost catches sunrise glory perfectly,
Scattering rainbow celebrations far and wide
Across snow-bright December landscapes where
Ordinary earth becomes holy ground today,
Sacred space in this Christmas morning light.

The day arrives robed in celestial splendor,
Yet gentle as a mother's tender touch still,
Blessing each waiting and wondering heart
With light that remembers deepest darkness,
With love that conquers every mortal fear.

* * *

BIRTH OF LIGHT

Afternoon

December sun reaches its Christmas fullness,
Pouring heaven's gold through parting clouds
That open like temple curtains drawing back,
Revealing glory's brightness streaming down
Through ordinary afternoon's blessed air.

Light streams through stained glass windows,
Painting ancient stories new in jeweled light
Across stone floors and waiting wooden pews,
While outside, winter sun transforms pure snow
Into fields of diamond-bright celebration.

The afternoon holds its breath in wonder
In moments suspended between all time,
Where past and future meet perfectly now
In present miracle, every sacred ray
A reminder of love's incarnate birth.

Christmas light fills empty spaces completely
With presence beyond all mortal telling,
Teaching us again how heaven touches earth
In common things made holy by this day,
How glory dwells in shadows transformed.

* * *

BIRTH OF LIGHT

Evening

Stars emerge like echoes of that first herald
That led seekers toward eternal truth revealed,
Each point of light becoming bright reminder
Of heaven's ancient and perfect promise kept,
Of love descending to transform our world.

Night comes clothed in celestial wonder,
Wearing constellations like jewels of memory,
While earth rests in starlight's gentle blessing
That speaks of love both human and divine,
Of light eternal breaking through our dark.

The evening deepens into pools of mystery
Where candlelight recalls that first night
When shepherds watched and angels sang,
When heaven opened its heart completely,
When Light came down to dwell with us.

Christmas night enfolds us in its blessing,
In mystery beyond all mortal speaking,
Where stars sing their ancient anthems still
And heaven's light continues leading us
Toward love's eternal dawning here.

* * *

BIRTH OF LIGHT

"For unto you is born this day in the city of David a Savior, who is Christ the LORD."

Luke 2:11

Reflections on the Day's Theme

_____

_____

_____

_____

_____

_____

_____

_____

_____

_____

_____

* * *

BIRTH OF LIGHT

Promise Fullfilled

Morning star burns bright
Heaven touches Earth with love
Light becomes our home

Advent Insight

The ancient tradition of lighting a new fire on Christmas morning symbolizes the divine light entering the world. Churches would carry this sacred flame into their communities, passing it from candle to candle, home to home, as a reminder that the light of Christmas is not meant to stay still—it is meant to spread endlessly outward.

Today's Call

As Christmas Day unfolds, notice how the light touches everything differently. Let each illuminated moment remind you that the light we've followed through Advent now lives within us, ready to shine through all our days ahead.

# # #

FINAL LIGHT

There are two ways of spreading light: to be the candle or the mirror that reflects it.

—Edith Wharton

As the final light of Advent shines, we are reminded that our journey doesn't end here. The hope we found in quiet mornings, the peace in still nights, the joy in shared moments, and the love that binds us all are the gifts we carry forward. Advent is not just a season; it is a way of being.

The Light was born in winter's deepest hour,
When stars held breath and darkness knew its end,
While shepherds watched and angels bent to earth,
A flame of hope no shadow could transcend,
Teaching us how heaven touches ground.

From dawn to dusk through Advent's sacred days,
We learned to read the language of the light:
In candle flame and frost-touched morning sun,
In star-strewn skies through longest winter night,
Each ray a promise carried in the heart.

Now as we journey forward from this place,
We bear this light through every waiting day,
Its warmth a testament to love's pure grace,
Its wisdom guiding others on their way,
Until all darkness yields to hope's bright dawn.

Carry the light of Advent with you into every moment and interaction. Let its hope inspire you, peace center you, joy uplift you, and love guide you. The journey begins anew, and the light you carry will illuminate the path for others.

For at one time you were darkness, but now you are light in the LORD.

Ephesians 5:8

SCOTT TILLEY

Rev. Dr. Scott Tilley is the founding minister and guiding voice of CTS Ministries, an emeritus professor at the Florida Institute of Technology, president of the Center for Technology & Society, president and co-founder of Big Data Florida, president of Precious Publishing, and a Space Coast Writers' Guild Fellow. His recent books include *Addictive Poetry* (2024), *Systems Analysis & Design* (2024), *Poems of the Moment* (2023), *AFTERMATH* (2022), and *PETS* (2021). He holds a Ph.D. in computer science from the University of Victoria. He can be reached by email at stilley@cts.today.

For more information:
- amazon.com/author/stilley
- linkedin.com/in/drtilley/
- www.CTS.today/ministries

 Ministries

CTS Upgrade Your Spiritual Life

www.CTS.today/ministries/join

PRECIOUS POETRY

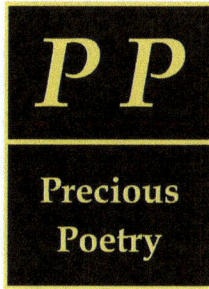

Words are important. Poems are the ultimate reflection of the art and craft of writing in a unique style designed by the poet and pleasing to the reader. Precious Poetry publishes books of poems that delight and refresh. If you want to assemble and publish a poetry collection, contact us!

Precious Poetry is an imprint of Precious Publishing, LLC. Precious Publishing specializes in taking your writing ideas from conception to fruition. We know that your stories are precious to you, and we'll do everything we can to help you see your work published.

All our books are available online from Amazon.com, usually in print and Kindle formats. You are the author, we are the editor and publisher, and the world's biggest bookstore is the global distributor.

http://www.PreciousPublishing.biz/PreciousPoetry